CW01019348

The Memory of Rooms

— Stride —

for Beverly

THE MEMORY OF ROOMS
New and Selected Poems

David H.W. Grubb

THE MEMORY OF ROOMS
First edition 2001
© David H.W. Grubb 2001
All rights reserved

ISBN 1 900152 74 6

Cover photo © David H.W. Grubb
Cover design by Neil Annat

Published by
Stride Publications
11 Sylvan Road, Exeter
Devon EX4 6EW
England

www.stridebooks.co.uk

Stride Publications
85 Old Nashua Road
Londonderry, NH 03053
USA

www.stridebooks.com

southwest arts

Contents

Writing on Silence   *13*

SELECTED POEMS

UNCOLLECTED POEMS

NEW POEMS

Writing on Silence

The poem as a device, both written and oral, carries an immense burden imposed by centuries of traditions and perceptions; it comprises an exceptional range of forms, an extraordinary usage embracing classic and orthodox to the most extreme experimentation. What we do with poems and what poems can do for us almost defies definition. The place of the poem maintains universal acceptance and yet of all creative acts it is often the quietest and most personal. Whereas in previous generations the hymn or the sermon became the vessel of the most precious human pronouncements, the poem is still an instrument of heightened expression and yet something not commonly admitted. Both the poem and the prayer can express our most significant statements and yet most find it best to keep quiet about such expressions. Sometimes the poem is so quiet it is almost silent.

Those who regard the writing of poetry as a serious undertaking work within a context of extreme pressures. Of all literary forms the poem is least likely to earn fame and fortune. The amount of poetry published and performed is naturally no guide to quality. A career in poetry is totally impossible for but a very small number. The death of poetry has been proclaimed for so long it might seem as if we are simply reading and hearing ghosts.

Despite all this, the real world still finds a place for poems. The public esteem for poets in South America, Russia, parts of Eastern Europe for example and the point when popular culture and literature merge as in pop song lyrics, indicate that certain values and recognition of the ability of words to amaze and influence survive beyond e-speak, jargon, sound bites.

The contemporary poet has therefore to define a place between the enduring, the influential, the fundamental, the experimental and the vast knowledge of what has gone before. It is this knowledge that is both essential and yet something that has to be surpassed as each new poem begins to demand its own right to existence, its own space. The audacity of the poet is therefore essential, to renew the energy, to give it another expression, to find a new voice, to speak as if nobody had ever heard this before. As the poem is read it transcends the descriptive to discover, the narrative is a revelation rather than only a reflection. Translation creates new understanding, the experimental goes beyond so that we behold differently; the communication of a poem lets in new light.

NOUMENON

The poem as an object of intellectual intuition attempts to identify what is most meaningful. It is the articulation itself that makes new meaning through a voice of discovery. As words so often undertake solely pedestrian communication, form is the essential dynamic in creating a view of the world, the self, new insight.

In many other art forms artifice is expected. The performance, the presentation, the sensations are exploited and it is anticipated that ordinary forms of communication will be surpassed. In the performing and plastic arts origination is vital in order to achieve a breakthrough. Fiction also adopts numerous forms and conventions so that at the very least the reader has points to build from. Perhaps it is because poetry has been so dominated by poetic devices and orthodox forms and also that these have been forced on to children from a very early stage, that the intuition is to hold to the traditional and deny contemporary poetics alternative forms of expression, radical regeneration.

On one level poems are examples of extreme device, artificial and magical because they are so different. They speak, say, relay beyond the normal. They let go of expected forms. They invent totally new energies. They thrust against perception and understanding and sometimes the complexity is astonishing and inspiring. They can also create such density as to confound the reader or listener and prevent any power of delight or discourse.

The poem is written to be said in the head and often read out loud. The look of the lines on the page, the form of stanzas, is designed to assist this special articulation. Fiction has dialogue and paragraph and chapter to order the transformations in the reader's mind. The poem on the page has to do more, it wants to. This distinctly denotes that this is a poem, this is poetic, this is not prose. The eye and the mind and then the meanings encounter music, magic of vocabulary, dexterity and the transforming core of the poem that creates something beyond any poetic form; poetry.

WHAT HAPPENS WHEN THE POEM IS BECOMING?

What happens when the poem is becoming? Collecting and releasing. Continuity so that the sounding of the voice in your being is attracting and discovering and opening out as the act of creating begins to settle out certain order and reordering and the expression begins. It is always an act of giving.

Sometimes this is a swift flow and one is almost overtaken by a voice and energy and the setting down of it. Other times one is aware of reordering, as if many times one had been at this task before, this tasking of self and identity and memory of words and idea of the thing coming into being.

There is all the time this sensing of being about this, of wanting to do it, now, getting it out and explored and refusing to formulate it too much in case the knowledge of other things begins to frame it too tight. The light needs to freely roam, encounter, occupy, even dazzle and beware the entrancement that may stop you too soon, fool you into thinking you have it caught there for ever. Always wait to be provoked again, a little further. Always await the subversive streak, the spill over into something else, the moment when what you beheld changes totally yet again.

What happens when the poem is becoming is a release from whatever has gone before, a leap that one had not actually planned, a transference from somewhere else, essentially a discovery so that this moment is more than rare, original, inspired.

What happens later will be about recognition, sensitivity, care and craft and a different knowledge but this follows, is not what creates initially. To do with values and text and understanding and whatever one gets from literature and other texts and other voices, yes; but not now, too soon, too close, too defining when what is essential is the opening, the wide light, the space given, the generosity, the laying out, the clearance, the hue of new.

What happens later is going to happen and always does happen but it does not itself make the creative moment happen. It may prepare, make aware, offer opportunity but it is never the orginator. This is why so much writing is a writing out of something already there, a renewal, a revisiting but not original. This is why and how the writer goes over and over and reads over and over and dwells so much on what it was when it was said. This is how we are all surrounded by other voices and texts and literatures and writing it out as if there could never be any escape. This is why there are so few truly original voices and unique poems and brilliant releases of light. Too much light to let us see the light. Too many singers to hear the enchanting one. Too much chasing the how and that stringent knowledge banging on our intellects.

The intuitive has to take hold and surpass our idea of form, literature, knowledge especially the task of writing. The angel of intuition will perhaps visit but rarely and the continuation of a writing career is therefore something like a preparedness, a keeping alert and fit for the actual moment of what Lorca called 'duende'. At that moment something is expressed quite beyond the words.

REFLECTING AND SELECTING

Selecting poems for this volume has been a matter of partnership between Rupert Loydell, poet, artist and publisher and myself. The notion that whilst one continues to write and publish and journey on, there may be some value in reflecting at a given point seemed attractive. On a more practical basis few readers will have read every poem before, texts get lost or are forgotten and this is one way of hopefully stimulating observations and questions about some of the most distinct output to date.

Is a 'Selected' meant to be the most representative, the most extreme, another narrative, a pooling of intuitions, a retrospective? Surely something more. This 'Selected' is chronological in terms of the actual date of publication in volume form. It is, therefore, representative of an individual collection at a given period and through the new poems provides a context of current endeavours.

During the process of reading over again and selecting I have been very much aware of the context of each piece of writing in terms of intuition, the impulse, the voice and the publishing history. A memory of the detailed properties of the poem naturally leads on to recollections of other things; what one was reading and hearing then, the publications and poetry readings, how the character on the page finally became the identity in book form. In this situation the merit of the writing is often overtaken by the memory of the creation and all those voices in other books, in the head, within the dialogues of definition and declaration and emotional demand.

There are, naturally, necessary repetitions, examples of concepts interweaving for years, life-studies that reveal themselves in both poetry and fiction, characters and characteristics. The committed reader often detects other things. There are also considerations relating to the poems that were extremely slow to reach completion, longer poems and sequences that normally come in a burst, the examples of lines that have haunted but only gradually found their best context, the enormous influence of people and places in the autobiographical poems, the immense emotional influence of the time I spent training as a psychiatric male nurse, the distanced and the displaced, the voices from war zones, the challenge to respond to atrocity and global terror refuting Auden's dictum. There also appears to be a considerable amount of God-spotting in these writings and more recently a sought for quality of light and silence.

The amount of poetry I read increases. I am a compulsive consumer of small magazines, individual collections, poetry on tape and CD. To hear Les Murray relishing as he reads his poems, to catch the discovery in Ted Hughes' voice, to feel the energy as Matthew Sweeney reveals and resonates enhances the possibilities of poetry. Then there are those other voices; William Carlos Williams, Robert Frost, Eastern European voices, those other dancers and drummers.

The amount of writing increases. There is no inhibition in perhaps having partly written it before. It all happens as if one had never drunk of this glass. It is intuitive; it drives one to write it out, it happens and gathers or disperses. Sometimes it is ill-defined or works at the bone of one's being for months, even years. It is like knowing a place that one has yet to visit. Incredibly this sometimes means that one writes a narrative and later it actually happens. Writing out a life becomes writing into a life.

The relationship between the poem and the prose is one of total continuity; in the case of many writers this is not so of course. It was so for William Carlos Williams and I find it interesting to reflect on how his career in medicine and his prose and poetry melded so precisely. Thus in my own writing, events, characters, visions and shades mingle and trace. At one moment the orchard, for example, is an entire poem, at another it is a single image but in my head and heart it is still the entire value. Is this perhaps another reason to gather a 'Selected'?

A 'Selected' is going to reveal several stylistic influences, many periodic shades and sounds. The greatest influences are likely to relate to positioning, subject, philosophy and not actual style. I know very well what W.G. Graham has alerted me to. I know what reading Peter Redgrove has 'given' me. I know what Wallace Stevens and Hart Crane created and wonder at its integrity. One's own voice and one's own life-material determine so much more, however. This is about owning the intuitive and when this is achieved the journey is radiated by specific shades and sounds.

•

This Preface gives me the opportunity to acknowledge the creative determination of several persons and publishers who have supported my work. They are partners in a tenacious tradition that currently embraces old technologies whilst in some cases pioneering the new. Their value is rarely recognised.

Such publishers work very hard with and for their authors. They display creative, design and production skills of immense range, versatility and merit. Rarely will their time and commitment be rewarded by financial success. With each new book they start again. From these small houses much of the major talent emerges and in many cases this is the only publishing outlet that will ever support the poets, the alternative, the experimentalists, the different voice.

There is today a vibrant alternative and minority interest in the U.S.A. and in parts of mainland Europe. In England poetry publishing is again on the periphery because of the fear of anything on the edge and 'literary'. If it cannot be marketed as the new rock and roll then it won't be published at all. The slim volume gets slimmer. Poets' deaths get mentioned, seldom their entrances, rarely their authority as change-agents, enhancers, entrancers.

David H.W. Grubb

SELECTED POEMS

from *The Green Dancers*

mud flats

flattened plots of nothing and the past
where old men chase lines and lines out to sea.
sea culled: the simple smear of slime towards a line.
shorewards: inky dells rimmed by broken bark strips.
further: dingles, weedmat rimmed and sharp grass
finger spread with vistas of slop puddles.
sea shot, sea spat, sea molten mud
that creeps crevices, peeks, then flattens rises.
slow sludge, omnimotional.

plots of nothing and the past.
rust freckled clutching anchors, green ragged;
pitched wood with rust-red burnt out bottoms
and ribs wrinkle wrecked in sad sand graves.
small fish folk, pie islanded or slime sunk,
swim round, or squirm, shell fans, chips and spirals.
thumb men in robber rows and sand-yolked mines
and fishermen like black oil devils who walk
in a place of nothing and the past.

ragged birds fly through white wind with
pipe-puff clouds and a somber smudged sun
over the plots of nothing and the past,
where young boys, unaware, finger flick fish.

from *The Burial Tree*

Tigers

Poetry is
        a shorthand
                to and from
                        the mind.

I approach
        in an unhesitating
                dance:
                        then stop

Hearing tigers
        lick the soft
                underbelly of
                        hidden fruits.

About Death

About death my Father has learned to be too kind;
stands there in his uniform of seagull white
knowing that black is the shade that brings them back
calling together cracking families
feeling that many will return only once again.

About death my Father has traded the textures
of fine white lies, standing so many times with
ashes in his hands, flesh flashing into the form
of hymns, cool grass creeping under the prayers,
following wild words right down into dark magnetic holes.

About death my Father has learned to use the easy ways,
stands here in church when a friend is dying after holy
communion, the breath melting away as I shove the dear man's
feet up and try to kiss back life, a lonely act, my Father
clasping the stiffening fingers praying too late
but honestly for healing hands.

About death my Father has constructed a moving staircase
down and up which his people must descend and rise,
and he will issue tickets in his uniform admitting
that there are no maps and no timetables and that
the signs are old but always there must be
places to go.

The Angels

The angels in our
                       church
Have given up
                  speaking

At night.

Somewhere in their
                    necks
They have tied up
                huge screams

Their thoughts
              grow webby.

Whispers burn holes in
                      the outbacks
                              of brains

Finger nails rattle
          the raw edge
                    of dreams.

One Hand Clapping
for Isadora Duncan
Memory of ideas

All she wanted
          to do
was see
          1,000 children running
down a
          long green hill to
Beethoven's Ninth:
                    in sunlight
too:

          but other things
              got in the way
                  like ignorance
                      and drink and
                          her body and
                          AGONY.

She should never have seen
the cracks in her dreams.

Farewell Fond World

The end came fast enough.
All we knew was thirst, all we
had to know was pain, up there on the hill
just out of the town's last happy view;
another tough old crucifixion scene, last
summertime and one great storm, resurrected,
revived to life, filmed for cash
and history.

Three trees, two thousand crowd,
beer and cigars, cars and crowds besides
Christian Christ with star dust on his toes,
bubble gum and a
bottle of Coke for
the Son of God &
'Christ Sleeps Here'.

Green stamps for John
for using so much gasoline, so many
girls, so many rides, so many nights out
he really did look tired; the
Virgin's wrap a competition prize
in some fat magazine,
another song:

> Cool Calvary: Were you there
> When our Lord
> Drove off
> In a Ford?

Dark eyed Judas running down our street,
the cigarette machines gone mad,
Pilate strolling in our town,
the motor boys
shouting
'Come on down'.

Only the guards were correct.
One more crucifixion take, pretend
you know the taste of mud and blood,
pretend you saw them blunt the nails,
pretend to forget the noise of nails on bone;
                        the wind screaming pain
                        wringing out rain
                        clutching cloaks of wild flame,
                        the Messiah's last moans
                        in a coiled tongue of film;
brought up in Boston
under New England leaves, dream of
a ball game and pretend you know.

Only the guards were correct...
                        This Cross was produced
                            by Harrison Woods
                        The Nails were presented
                            by Thomas Legree
                        This Cross was erected
                            by David Contractors
                        The Hillside was covered
                            by local TV...
relaxed and bored; who said the hardest thing
to act was being bored?
Only the guards knew how to take it,
crouching low,
playing cards.

Tree with Apples and Without

Try to understand the apple tree
Not the apples because they will only
Last the year snug in the cellar
In straw, some of them on the sideboard at
Christmas shining and polished to a
Foreign perfection.

Study the tree not the fruit though
The taste is beautiful fresh and good
And each apple in the hand is tempting
Wants the pleasure now the big ones too
Large and still green in parts and the
Small ones sweet and quick and numerous.

Study the arms that will be here all
The year of the Autumn and Winter and again in
Spring the same green song that is always coming and coming
And coming back again always working through what seems on
A Winter's wet day hard and death-touched wood that will never
Be able to do it again; but does.

Take the tree itself that may outlive you &
Certainly is not alone in the world so much as
Humans are, so much as birds are, hardly seen alone
But has no motivation that we can speak of save its
Own tough religion of vigour and insistence, its own
Devotion of discovery that leaves us standing under its
Arms slightly awkward and always amazed.

And this is good for us: awkward with the ladders
Scared of the height sometimes and half guilty thinking
Of greed more than of Mr. Adam and what he and his first wife did,
Taking the baskets in, lined with straw, taking the apples and sometimes
The twigs at the stalks, worm-like, down down down paths that are grassy
Into the dark of homes.

And outside, still there, the robbed tree: pleasure in it
Still, persistence of it,
That we know and love but never explain.

Two Old

It is hard to think
Of them making love.
Small trees have
Grown sturdy
Whilst they have lived,
Whilst they have lived,
Stars frozen a fraction
More, pews slimmed
by centimetres.

When they were both young
He hunted in the forests
Of her hot body,
Their words were
Birds.

Now they are old
She has horse-bag breasts,
His chin is like a soap bar,
Their bodies are ruins
Turning to
Still stone.

Chairs face each other
At different angles
Of gathering
Silence;
Words are warnings
They do not sing or shine
Or they are blunt weapons,
They are sounds
Without feeling;

When they kiss
They are dying
Their lips are
Cool as cork.

It is hard to think of
Them making things;
But they have:

A world
        for
            ever.

Angels

Suddenly
        our sky is filling with them
White
      of cool fire
                    silent lightning
                                thunder birds.

All over
        the place
                    is becoming
Their circus:
            doors opening
                            traffic stopping
                                            roof tops
                                                    filling up
ROOFTOPS
CAMERAS
REPORTERS
INTERVIEWS
CROWDS

WINDOWS
ROOFTOPS
'OFFER THEM A DRINK'

                    filling up
                         and down
                              and along
                                   and across

Car parks
          getting crowded
                    as well
                         with folded wings.

Loudspeakers
               and bells
Proclaim
          the invasion
                    trees hold hands
                         as the sky collapses
                         in a radiant rain...
Customs and tax men
               are wracking their brains
          'WHERE ARE THEIR PASSPORTS?'
          'THERE MUST BE A FORM; SOME FORM
                    OF A FORM.'

Priests confess confusion
                    'GIVE THEM SOME BREAD.'
'STAND BACK THERE.
                    STAND BACK.'
                              the army
                              moves
                              in...

The Burial Tree
& other ideas

1

'The mind must move in the intention of LOVE.'
Always the changes are slow
A man's ambitions trail on his living
There are easier ways, cruder codes,
But the changes are real,
The chances are Hope.

> I have seen women
> with beautiful hair,
> bright red hair, waves
> of a flame, but
> the dreams that they
> fall through are
> slabbed with cold stone
> deep in their eyes are
> the tigers of death.
> At the dancing contest

Lorca saw
Women and girls with 'waists like water'
But a woman of eighty carried off the prize,

> in her soul
> the dark spirit,
> in her body
> DUENDE.

2

You have a bird that
stays with you grown
tame with kindness:

For six days now it
takes you food but
every hour it
moves to death:

the changes exist
the chances gain

        The burial tree
        is a singing tree
        is a climbing tree
        it looks so green.

3

That
old man
is always happy.

He has six strong sons
with six healthy wives
who will cook for him
and comfort his limbs
and bury him properly when
the sun burns his bones: he

        is very happy: intellect fed
        by (dis)
        grace of the belly.

4

In the Lao Tzu
a performance of attitudes
designed against
the unkind mind
and certain death

        and Confucius planned
        a code of living
        so after life
        there is nobility
        in death:

                        both old men
                        with dreams in their bones.

5

The Walk

            is not with fire or thunder
                rock or bird song the women dancing
                    the women with earrings always dancing
                        the old man ruled by the voice of the deep
                            god in his groins faith in his food or
                                women who sleep wrapped in their hairs
                                or the hunters who raise their bows to
                                THE MOON:

the change is in all things; death is

                            a

                    movement.

6

She died so suddenly. At Christmas time.
A taxi came. The driver smoked a dirty pipe
And drove his dragon through the city fog.
The house was damp. The lights had gone.
My Mother lit a cracked and dusty candle.
The flame danced up and licked a trail of web
Then settled down to light up yellow faces.
The bedroom smelt of flesh and soup.
A doctor came to cross two hands, close
One eye. The right lid wouldn't fasten.

7

If I die before
remember that it was
this winter
I wrote a poem for you;

but it was no good
and you only saw it
(came into it)
when it was on fire

the ashes, you said
were white
like
'wings of moths'.

8

Between first dawn and last,
a life. Between first turn and last turn and
the drive,
memory: the conversations of lawnmowers, the peace
of paths and trees, artificial flowers and real ones,
stone angels and weeds: My mother and
My Father moving in slow-motion
black gigantic thunder birds.

Just for You

Sun
        a misty piston-ring
Pools
        nervous nudes;
                        your
Words were birds
                nesting
        in air.

And Suddenly, This

Waiting for sun we did not
expect snow so late this year
coming after I had cut the lawns;
unusual as clowns
at funeral services.

Pussy willow is out. Lilac is
rushing snow. The rake cleans
through last year's ruins. Not all
birds wait for deep-green privacy.

Waiting for sun I did not
expect you to mention death:
leukaemia. It grabbed at him
at school. I wonder how we
mourn with love.

A settling of it for half
an hour. The buds bound up
in stiff respect. I photograph
a silver web. This poem grows
up.

Wings

Father; sometimes the wings you build
collapse. You won't admit it; hums and fumbling
filling the lonely spaces. Mother helps you straighten
out a stream of strings. And then,
you're off again.
'Icarus was there,' you say:
and I believe you.

I've known you practice in your room
all night. You fly below the moon, aim for
the sun one day. Mother helps you when you crash;
leads you back to bed, brings you matches.
'Icarus will learn in time,' you say, smoking your
pipe, patting the sheets. You stare at the light.
You can't make up your mind what's wrong.

Later, you try again; then sleep.
My mother runs a glass of water, walks about
the drifting room. I hear her muttering, planning
how to patch up wreckage, picking up your shirt and
twisted tie and
broken wings.

Later she switches off the light, perches
her chair in the ribs of the dark, rocking;
and weeps.

My Evangelical Grandfather and Balloons

The way they 'rose to Heaven'
attached to children's hands
attracted him; a notion of string,
the frailest contact being enough
to keep them here
on earth.

He was a humble man who always
smelt of soap and dressed in black
making his skin white as an
unsung psalm; even his ears
had dignity and when he smiled
his eyes caught
shafts of glass.

He called me simply 'the boy'
and died before I learnt to
doubt his god. It must have led
to years of carefully tapered
steel, I think. He would have
forged some hope with thoughts
of that day at the fair in
Kent; a Saturday evening and
God loomed over the flashing
swings.

There was no time to stay
between the ghost train screams
and rifle shots and bowls of prisoner
fish and so he bought us gay balloons
and hardly took his eyes off one as we
walked home;
red and loud,
            bright as a lie.

A Suspension

'Everything imagined is reality...
The mind cannot conceive unreal things.'
        David Smith, American Sculptor.

There can be no edge to this
if it is good:
            anecdotes in air,
                    clutched conversations with no sounds,
the central dispute with folds of meaning
making other forms
and more: a
god's groin cracked to
                    fractured totems.

His great hope had been to make a
   'sculpture that would rise from water
      and tower in the air...'

          to race into
sky's steel, wind's scar-tracks:
the world's junk jaws,
      turnbuckles flanges harrows brackets
big as a meadow in July.

Carpenter, window designer, telephone lineman;
once, as a cabbie, a bit of a dandy
'would drive his cab wearing spats, wing collars and
carrying a cane.'

braze   silver-solder... arc-weld with iron:
draw cup spin forge chisel grind file... polish
with steel:
     he felt the stones of the planets
'arriving at form.'

May was like a ragged madrigal;
      urgent, attentive, bolted
to moon:
     damp as the silence of stick and bone:
          in 1965
his pickup truck went off the road:
       draw
       cup
       chisel and grind:

he was crushed to death
near to his
home.

For Jane Austen on a Rainy Day
in Blinking Spring
Her tired events.

I will give you a dance
to measure beneath
a thumb of
moon.

Darkness is a
quality.

I will alter all the
door knobs. I will change
the cities of the sun.
I will stick new candles
beneath the lids
of graves.

After the first dance
I will revise
all my
clothes.

Good horses for good
dancers – to take
them home.

'We were too
magnificent';
often we filled large
ballrooms with
small ideas.

Your notion of hell
is a damp
card room.

The passages of hell
were sometimes built
between hallways
of
        sudden sun.

Heron Feeding

'Take it easy. Stand still.
Be led by event.
Bank your reflexes in shallow
waters; listen and watch.
Nothing comes of hurrying;
efficiency and patience are
the properties of
perfect murders.
Gradually, if you have to, move
forward, then wait,
for fish flick, eel ripple, frog
flop, or the hollow damage
of the vole.
They do my work for me.
Small fish I swallow whole;
head first, one gulp:
only the large ones take
up time; stab by stab
I clean their bones.
Take it easy. Water is
the wine of time.
Destruction is a deliberate
industry, mirrors of violence
dissolving upon landscape's
instinct.
Be certain.
Be slick.
KRORNK. KRORNK.
KRORNK.'

Owls

Often
we see these birds
inhabiting corners of night,
judge-hunched in hurt air
or stretching corridors of
moon:

we sense what they are attempting,
what gristle attracts, how
lightening gets into
the tares of their eyes:

they would do nothing
but doom-watch over us, making
our night rides journeys of doubt:

refusing to look beautiful
they contemplate sharp magic;
refusing to sing
they cannot forget
what has not been:

scurrilous senators
they have tasted the urine of
history, they have sensed the ruined
membranes of
                    the moon.

Silence is a Distance

1

Hang it all, Gertrude Stein, there is only one PASSPORT:
silence.
Let the crabs of your mind settle in dark corners;
be constant.

2

I heard night fall between the heights
of tired elms.
I stood in the cage of the wood
waiting for dogs to bark in the
village.
I waited a long time
hearing my breathing
like the unseen
bleeding
of enormous
oaks.

3

Words fall out of their skins.
I inspect them carefully beneath an
expensive microscope:
the sly ticks, the triggers and tricky
mechanisms, the covered-over
wounds:

one incision and you might discover something incredible:
two incisions
and it's
dead.

4

The distance is
air

& those things that live in the
air

elements of silence,
the pure propaganda of its
realms.

Rain comes down across the minds of poor people
and the things that live in air

(slim births and deaths
and intervals
and perhaps even wars)

& those things that persist in the
air.

Silence is those things that inherit the
distance.

The Glass Sun
for Stevie Smith

When I grow old
said the lion
I will travel to a strange land
and eat the meat
of seven seas
when I grow old.

When I grow wise
said the lion
I will wear the sun's crown
and give my words
to those who cannot
dream:
when I grow wise.

When I am dead
said the lion
you will hear my attendants
slowly dancing
before mirrors
of
broken moon:

remember the tune.

To Preserve Territory

To preserve territory
define what possession is
hang pictures of war lords
on the walls
spread butter with swords
always carry a plan for invasion
in your pocket
examine the triggers of rose buds
divide your bed into separate theatres
examine the seams to your dreams and
give your wife a Berlin Wall.

To preserve territory
define what obsession is
give away your weekends
your caravan holidays
your coach trips and tents and
castle tours
allow dust to take over the dustbins
permit your living room to
gradually die
and walk with the dead.

To preserve territory
examine the sad wills of tortoises
define what the third testament never
said
listen to the slow claws of glaciers
the gradual howling of the moon
keep a third eye centred on the
back of your best friend's
friendliest
lies.

It is all meant for you:
all the mirrors in all the halls of all the
mansions that have never been:

the centre of the fire
                    is rose.

A Galaxy Within
(6 Notes for Winter)

Note One

I have been thinking about stars, water, stones
since reading Lao Tzu: a galaxy within.
And of pathways
and decisions
against going anywhere at all.

Note Two

Your letter about Vietnam
and your great friend
forced to the beer tents each evening
deeply depressed me: he has to be born again:
is it true that all people have to be crucified
by their own lives;
each war replaced by the love of a woman?

Note Three

We are building another wall.
It is to be made of slate.
We are virtually
controlling
a natural
event.

Note Four

To begin it again: the axe
lodging just outside the knot, splitting
down more easily, the force and the nervous
beauty of the grain.
To begin it this evening, the clocks all cold
as onions, the supper warming, the axe sounding
from the yard, evenings stretching out so that
one can work far far longer.
The axe raised and the idea of another year
four weeks old; chipped off.
A telephone call about insurance.
Cold proposals of morning's ice.
Poems gathering into this book
of seamless ideas.
Children running past the gate from school;
of all things
blowing bubbles.
The bubbles rise up
into an old thatch
itchy with birds.

Note Five

Sometimes it is good to just
stare at it; different appearances
from window
lawn end
the far point:
it is going well
this wall building:

it could last
100 years.

Note Six

Stone gives far less than wood
in creation. Its frozen centre
must be left untouched
or it will explode.
Naturally
it will give birth
to numerous smaller
creations
each with its own centre
if there is any
vigour
at all.
Understand this
and
you can never die.

Seven Scenes for Paul Klee

1

The sun inside
the sea inside the
moon inside the secret
garden inside the angry gates
inside the broken star inside nine
hours of snow: and
suddenly
tree gets up and walks

                   away.

2

An old man
sitting in a garden of nettles
on a wooden bench sitting between
apple blossom
falling on his dark blue suit
sitting beneath another sun
inside another day
and memory
like the face of a friend
through a broken pane
of ancient
          glass.

3

At the funeral
one umbrella is green and
one bicycle is red and one
man gets his fingers caught
in the door
of one of the cars
and his voice grabs
at the air:
for one moment we forget
and only see what it does
to the sky.

4

The deck chair
is in the sun.

5

The thin man's
hump-backed
                    submarine-slick
sentences
plonking like rabbits on cold glass
all the way
to the grave of meaning:
fat man (in a blue top hat)
lets the words escape
sly butterflies
                    that are doomed
breaking before you see them out
                              of sight.

6

The umbrellas
in shafts
of
      sudden
            mooooooooonlight.

7

The sun
inside
the
old man
sitting
inside
the
      voice.

Playing. Out in the Fields
of Somerset. In Snow.

One of the best games ever was
pulling out the old funeral cart.
Once a boy from a farm was brought
in for his burial on a waggon, cleaned
and painted-up and stacked with flowers;
but this was the real vehicle, wheels with
spokes of flashing doom and a long whip of
a handle and a terrible unexpected smoothness.
We hardly rode on it but carried out imagined
cargoes: raging slaves, screaming saints, dying
kings.

One time, in snow, we set it rolling in the
fields and sent it off alone roaring down
towards the stream. It cut the field in two
and rocked and jumped before it slowed and
some old fellow came and shook his fist and
swore at us for fooling with the instrument
of God.

We towed it back, the snow still clinging
to its record of a race against expectancy.
It was as if we'd drawn out signs with
charcoal wands; and after that the mud,
and after that a place the grass refused
to grow.

Nothing Comes
(Cornish Farmer)

Nothing comes like this;
winter returns to the land
and all night you dream
of the onion eyes of sheep,
mist like an ancient whisper
and earth, earth.

Listen; you will never understand
earth, dark flesh made fertile, trees
and hedges that are essential.
Lying in bed at night,
ideas licked away by darkness,
you must realise how
it is slowly killing you.

But what else is there?
You spend entire days trying
to forget the sea, heckle of gulls,
blunt refusal of your body
to take to waves;

and the towns; acres of iron,
clean stones and
crops without roots.

Listen; the cold wind catches
your sense and shapes stone
of cottages and walls and the
sad wood of closed doors:
all your life
picking over the dark resurgence
of desperate days:
you will never understand this,
but nothing else
will ever come.

Mrs. Coldlove's Reply

Are you happy?
The birds on her dress
move a little as she breathes.
She looks toward the sun and
remembers sitting on a beach
in Italy once. The man selling
sponges was nice to her. The zoo
near her house makes happy noises
at night. The pub is a good place
in winter. Somewhere in her body
there's an album of happy events.
But to answer the question; a ripe
rose, the roots of a summer field.
The dream of what a first night might
turn out to be. A virtue in the challenges.
But to make a real reply.
A window collapses and glass over the grass
is again a window in the sun.
A dead man is measured in the event of his
death by his life, in his going. Death just
won't ever leave us alone, etc...
Of course, of course.
Walk on the glycerine folds of the sea.
Record the music of a hare's screaming
as it is bitten to death. Fish out the
night's deep-rivered plankton. The zoo
near her house is nearer every year;
too much nearer. She would choose a hill
to make a reply. She would choose a hill
to answer the sun. She would tell me all
her truths there, everything there is
there. Age fingers the skin under her
eyes. It is an awkward movement. It is
a message riddled with lies. Yes.
She would like to be able to run.

Four Night Songs

1

Everything is possible in the night songs.
We make love. We listen to the dark and what
night inherits. I tell you
about nights when I was young and a fear of
thunder. You also thought of beggarmen and
tramps alone in rain
and in that film
we saw in Spain
lighning in the eyeballs of the truly mad.

2

The Holy Man, always there at birth
and death. Navajo Indians taking
the newly born to be baptised;
sprinkling them with corn pollen
and talking of sun. And yet we
make love for ourselves and
do not talk of gods.

3

I was writing late. I was scared
to open the words out onto
the page.

4

The song of the night is harmony.
The trees of our dreams get up; they
are getting up to dance. Stones move
into new patterns.
An old man in a field
is teaching his horse
how he can sing.

From the White Room

(Psychiatric Hospital. Winter)

1

Arrangements, decays, the unsung days
collapsing on their own
intervals:

and we get here by failure to reach
anywhere else
or a position that might
otherwise be stated:

to the white room, the open never closing room
that skids on its own
perception.

2

Getting nowhere we remain still
and travel all over the place
aware of what others cannot see
but state they know
hearing the big bird of understanding
mate in the dark with
fat deceit.

3

From the white room
through huge windows
to winter and the grass
beneath snow. In

summer they push out the beds onto that grass
and we learn to die beneath remembered
evergreens.

4

The man who smashed the Madonna
faces a white sheet in the art room, hears
blue music from the radio, waits for the hinge
of memory to swing. In

the vase there are five snowdrops. They are the
sweat of angels, the secret rain, the dead dew. They

interpret what cannot be loved in conception. They
arrange cool intervals
for the Madonna to smile.

5

From the white room you hear
what cannot be said. You receive the visitors you
do not know. They tell you they love you. They speak their
invisible tones. They arrange their festivals of summer

lies.

6

The best time in the white room is night time; you
hear in the morning of the three o'clock deaths and you
hear yourself blessing the wind. Leaving the window of the mind
half open.

7

In the white room you forget the future; present and past
come together like tired old professors: they sit down in the
white room and wonder how they cannot see the deaths of others.
Unanswered questions turn to snow.

Inside the Instituion

Two of the things I saw inside
the institution, apart from the
man waiting for Mary, apart from
the woman who stroked the chairs,
was the African male nurse who
danced on the table at his first
view of snow, was the old mad man
one evening of the following spring
bending over a potted bulb:

> Where do you go?
> Where could you come from? he said.

and the man still waits for Mary
and the woman still strokes the chairs
and they never were dead.

Blue Ice

You are the one we do not talk about. Your room
at the end of the corridor is forever silent except
for the sobs. We can't take it. You could scream and curse
or throw your food around or mess the sheets and somehow
we'd measure this against your sick distress: but silence,
and the slow sobbing like the bleeding of a tree.
Grey, small-failure man, moony-man, blue bruise-man;
how to make you out. You take our food and as I shave your
slippery chin the tears roll down straining cheeks.
Snow must have stacked inside your skull; perhaps blue ice.
For thirty years you've rested on this drift:
I wonder, now, how you will let us know when you are dead.

Hearing the Music
Three Songs for My Grandfather

1

My grandfather
walks on the lawn.
It is autumn and
sermons lie in his mind
like stone leaves.
He remembers the first one,
touching the fine cordage of
love, hearing the music,
fumbling for the ability
to sing. Sixty years later
it is about the same. Time
falls down on its knees
and love is the murmur of
mountains. He sees the world
is smiling and thanking him
for something he knows
he has not done.

2

My grandfather walks
on the autumn. The lawn
and sermons lie in his mind
like stones remembering.
Leaves touched by the fine
cordage of love hear
the music, fumbling
sixty years later or
the ability that is
about to fall to its
knees. Love is the mountain's
murmur. He sees the years have
done something he does not own.

3

My grandfather walks on
the memory. Fumbling for
the years he sees things
he does not own
about to fall.
His mind touches
mountains
and love is
the hearing, the music, the
sermon:
ability.

Departures

All of the young years with the old. On dry Saturdays
driving with my father to the old people's home, sitting
in front of those sad smashed-fruit faces with the seconds
collapsing all round us. Everything they said was stolen.
Everything they hoped was dead. The harmonium in the chapel
and the dribbly lips as they sang and the fat one always
wanting to kiss me as we left. As she hugged me I smelt the
loaded sweat and sensed a jolt would pull the sockets out
and let the rusty hair and mossy flesh rub my cheeks.
One of them died one day as we were walking out. She let the
life slip from her like a finished book. I was amazed at the
way the others refused to panic; smiling slowly, offering more sweets.

Imitations

My child imitates the wind. My child imitates the bird.
She watches the small ones trying their flights and sees
the sun and moon in the same sky these days in May with
the garden buzzing. She goes to sleep within the green of it,
the deep sleep with the poppy heads swaying in night garden,
new seeds steadying in soil; ceremony of accuracy to be noted
in delight and those sudden smiles. And when she rolls on the ground,
when she rages, I think this is more a part of me than the world;
I think she imitates my broken faith and dances night dance
and learns the less than accurate despair of clowns and tramps
and lost men everywhere who want a house to crawl inside, who
are an animal, who are an itch; living imitations of lasting ice.

The Priests of Wessex

The priests of Wessex love the wide days of summer
when the wind is a white horse with a happy rider
and the mystery is calmed by green fields and high
flying laughter. There is space then to forget the
scars, the deep animal blood, the movements that cannot
let this land alone. It is not ghosts or the yelp of
legend or that soul of the wilds that Hardy found on
Winfrith Heath so much as the people, the same people,
returning with face maps bearing that sad skin of
testimony, that native dream that cannot be taken or
destroyed. It is as if some moth kingdom of the mind still
operated within them, some territory rare as a Lulworth
Skipper, druid-hunched, remembering. And the priests with their
modern answers and swift God cannot get there. The church
exists with winter bells. Evenings come with ancient suns
eating the latest definitions. Lichen packs the eyes of
small stone creatures making them blind in sun, blinking
back darkly in the months of hard rain. And the priests
keep their conversations short, carry those dry official

smiles, wishing they were poets. They have become improbable
messengers or staggering servants in a land of fabulous code.

from *Somewhere There Are Trains*

Sequences for Wallace Stevens

1

And the earth gets to where it has to
and the positions do not remain the same
and what is said is another style of chance.

2

So many of the sad things might have come
other ways. Countries with clipped understanding
and miracles too common to be recognized.

3

And I did not ask for this. Before birth the area
hardly considered. After death and a fear of
deceit or defeat or what is it?

4

Land teaches us nothing. Order and confusion
and the cultural reflexes. The skin of things
to be constantly alive.

5

Performance and attitude. How long do
your worries get before you reject them?
So many crowns and crowds of doubts.

6

What is absent travels with us just the
same. A returning of something not there
but possible in the mind's extension.

7

Order and rejection. Analysis as the operation
and the healing conclusion. And finding nothing,
and finding something all these years.

8

Quietly. Considerately. Or the wall-rushing
painful burning. Identity as a smashed toy
soldier and gods collapsing to their knees.

9

And no-one asked for this. We came, made
doubts and gods. Gave a fraction back.
Grew used to these helmets of living dust.

10

There are no other ways of doing this;
each man gets out, gets up, dances
and breaks his legs beneath the sun.

11

Time and the gods; old things constantly
hatching back. A fresh way of embracing
the lie. A new moon and a new truth.

12

Certainly one has become more aware of the
stature of events. We are better at death
and less good at dying.

13

And the old protections of love, the protocol
of honesty. The young with sun under their
skins and the burning grass.

14

These things do not travel easily.
I own more and more. Materials conceive.
I give you less and less.

15

Walking on the water is part of a miracle;
there have been greater things. It is the memory
and survival that is a wonder.

16

Nothing would reward the old gods now. They
would die on a heap of ruined harvests. They
would fail to recognise their own prophets.

17

The brain unravels the clock backwards.
The law of things bulges and gets smaller.
You catch a star and crucify a human.

18

Nothing travels so well in the memory as
tough reality. The token wobbles, falls over
and a doubt falls out.

19

What does not change is the seed and its
changing, is the water in its rewarding, is
rock history and the dent of event.

20

And the earth gets to where it has to
and the positions do not remain the same
and what is said is another style of chance.

from *Falconer*

Falconer Looks Through a Book of Old Thunder

Bone man was his father
with stone dawn and early rip of memory; man
with pain in his face, eating meat raw, swallowing
sun that he owned. Put a cage round a mountain and called
it life. Hacked out a blunt idea and kissed it until it bled.
Built a circle and made love to it. Almost killed the baby
by feeding it earth. Then words. Time bent to the index of fear.
A sense of belief. He watched the tree and the baby grow.

Flesh woman was mother;
the breast filled with memory and fingers
to play with. She hit him into life, ached him into action;
gave him a river for his birthday, a rat as his toy.
One day she climbed the tree and fell into a space
called death. They gave her body to the lion.

Inside the book he see the man, the woman, the tree, the suns:
he see the stone under the snow:
he see the fox attack the bat:
he see the tree bend into moon:
he see the silence that was love:
he see the words that got through:
he see the face of the face of the fear:
he see the sound of the shadow of space:
he see the warnings like a head full of puss:
he count the eagles
as they fall
from the sky.

Bone man
is broken time
is marriage in the mind:
flesh woman is slow river
running into night: baby
is sound in the sense of the storm.

Falconer's Winter Game

Winter; bone territory: sky wider than event.
Old water in the distant seas that he never
visited now; valleys like fists in snow skins.

He observed. Bell bruise from their churches,
small stones to cover the dead; death in
the earth like soaked secrets.

A music that was different, a ritual unity or
sense of answering in this questioning, these
songs that were decreed.

Memory pack: old tale; Jesus Boy; the scream
in the green garden and Christ with spider
blood: a miracle to stuff inside the world's
big mouth.

Memory. Praying for the dead to stay where
they are, for old stone to stay still; for the
black angels to keep to the hills.

Not knowing what was known angered him. Sad
Aprils came, came with sea wreck and ice
giving away. Floods.

And it mattered. It was one thing that they
might have defined for him more than their wars
and orders and logic of territory.

But the Book that he stole was silent rain
the prayer that he aped was dud machine
the rain that he ran to was a terrible hole.

Falconer Waits

He had said this. He
had these messages made inside his mind
and sent through January snow. This season was
ice and ready for innovation. He had packed the year
inside a cold memory and sworn to give away the stone
eggs. The stone eggs were not worth keeping. They would
lead to misunderstanding: grass betrayal: wind spite: no.

He had said this: to bent river, bad eye of time, old ruin
of rock, tall tree that the wind failed to take: hurt of his
winter home: and now he waited
for the girl to come.

Without the girl he would sell the cave. The estate agent had
smiled. His suit perhaps was wrong. The agent had smiled and tried
to sell him an island. He had smiled back. An island was a good idea.
The island sat within the picture within the sun within the beach view
near to the sea and the gilt edged security was delivered by a girl
dressed in neat skin.

Falconer waited for the plans to arrive and the buyers to arrive and
the girls to arrive: he had a gift for her: wrapped in a year's web
it was his soul.

The wind had yellow teeth.

It laughed again.

Falconer's Word Game

Cannot be snow, said Falconer. Old helmet mated in earth. Sea scrawl on tired glass. And where is the memory?

Time settles in stone. Small creatures take over the ruined trees. Swollen letters postpone sudden years.

I cannot live outside these words. They dance with me. Time zips them into tidy festivals.

The dead are whispers.

And When He Climbed into His Death

And when he climbed into his death
it was not neat trees and faces like comfortable moons
but voices
that told him he should not die
must not die
there were things to do still to do to be done still:

he had never been so happy in his death.

from *Last Days of the Eagle*

The Dead Owl Poem

I give a dead owl to the priest.

He says all life has expected this.
Satisfactory as a state funeral or
the view of summer remembered in
January. On the other side of the
psalm is memory. On the other side
of memory there is nothing.

I give a dead owl to the teacher.

Give it back to the sky he shouts.
The long night wants this. Coming across
events like these warns us about short
journeys. I keep these things in a book,
in a hollow, in a chapter of night.

I give a dead owl to the soldier.

He is silent. This is expected of him.
The city gets up and tells the rain to fall
silently. The sun dances on the dead men's
brains in small, grey countries. Only a
military man can make sense of nonsense.
History jabbers from the soldier's badge.

I give a dead owl to my mother.

She clothes it in ideas. She buries it in
words. Her sounds press out the wrecked
feathers. Her memory folds neatly what is
broken. She goes to the library and finds
the big bird book and reads it to the dead owl.

The Dreamer Jumps Out

for John Berryman

John Berryman dies; falling through broken reality
is the stunted song, the way of outdoing irony at its
own barbed game. He dies and a friend reads a poem in his
memory and fails. There cannot be another
place like Berryman's mind. It can only be an attempted
grace. Each man makes his own borrowing of references.
Occasions like this cheat us; we mirror-index what seems
momentous and it becomes casual. We chase these ghosts
of the great and skate over the merest reflexes. We are
left with small duties as we can find them. Water and air
and stone change in our minds. Conclusions catch us out;
the same winds mould us; we are our own winter prophets.

Through Glass

After we had decied to buy the house, after the decision of
words, after visits to that garden ruin and questions of
territory and a visit late at night with moon on the single
pear tree;

after documents of tears, silk screen of values, distemper
of negotiation, we hung up our hopes and dressed reality in
a sudden uniform that we hardly believed.

We removed a ceiling and discovered joists. We removed five
layers of wallpaper and used white paint. We removed wind
from the garden and planted.

The upstairs window bore scratches we thought
a child must have made. We wanted some small grey creature
caught in a slow arc of moon to moan at the window with
the beasts of mad parents hunched in the seeding dark, in
the ranting black; or a hunched lady working a blade across
glass trying, trying always to describe a lover she had never
known.

After three years we discovered the village mid-
wife had lived here. At night villagers came to
throw stones at her window to bring in the life.

Hers was the pear tree and the garden that took our days
each summer.

How to Bury the Night

In one country they will come with silences and white boxes.
They robe the night with songs and carry it away. It is left
by sea.

In another country they give it a book to read. The pages
bang. Words jump like babies. Confused, it crawls into the
ears of the dead.

If you are unlucky
in certain parts of this universe you can see poor people
eating it. They think it is a certain food. They prepare for it
carefully reserving midnight for their gods.

In Cornwall it is cursed and placed beneath stones. In Wales
it is asked to tell a joke. In Spain they try to make it dance.
In Iceland it fornicates in late July. It has flowers.

The Shakers of Niskeyuna

In formal photographs they look like God's farmers,
those 'inherited' children promising regeneration
like borrowed miracles.
The days are bound tight by prayer power;
the sun has permission to be here.

It is a 'wheel dance'.
The aged and infirm sit it out on hard benches
with the fat beast, the rage rogue, dead in them.
Their flesh is forgotten rivers;
there is no rhythm can drain them now;
their bodies are sermon shadow hung up to die.

Beneath a vaulted ceiling the spirit gets its kicks;
women at the centre, flesh becomes a testimony of
stinging sweat, lust runs on the floor its ruined dragon stains:
the 'wheel' groans its ghosts.
Hang the chairs up, dust the days,
scrub the sky, seal down regret:
sin is trodden in
like a black-brained hound.

One woman becomes a human wind bag, a holy hoop.

from *Mornings of Snow*

Waiting for Words on a Long November Day

Walking by sea I hear the dark knights of the universe
plotting their suicidal dreams. They have sold their memories
to Hollywood professors. They have sold their deceits to the
scientists. They have sent off their ideals in small packing
cases to neat addresses with easy zip codes. Now in the night
of their minds they try to recall small children, mornings
of snow, long distance elegies.

Waiting for words on a long November day mice enter the gobs
of dear giants, the king begs the tutting turtle to remember
him, old women are put to sleep by weeping dolls
and bell ropes coil in helpless air
waiting for faiths.

from *The Mind and Dying of Mr Punch*

Punch Hears Music from Mr. Elgar

Pompous and circumcised and true-blue
in a red-striped blazer. The summer lawns
cut just right. The flowers in good order
and the hedges helping to protect an English
garden in its correct perspective.
Not one dog or lady or deck chair out of place.

And the afternoon nodding off, gently reclined, inclined
to the taste of cucumbers and sipped tea and
freshly-cut conversations. 'Of course. Just so.
Quite naturally.'
The very slightest motion towards evening and dress
for dinner and appointments with momentous
circumstantial perspectives.

Punch, having been politely clapped by all the children
and their wooden hands, is flung back into his grave-
shaped box.
The afternoon gently leaks. The conventions are
surrounded by music from Mr. Elgar.
He is so well known, so English.
He is so important.
He is playing 'Happy Birthday To You'.

Punch Considers the Man Again

The crowds are getting smaller. This must be
his fault, his error, his crooked deals.
Nobody wants to hear that voice anymore.
A dead cat-rant and jokes as old as Moses
and the infant symbolism slipped in like
a sleeping pill.

Sod him; fat brain, slow hands, same old tyranny,
same old litter of fables.
Punch would like to rape the wife and kiss
the crocodile and live with the little child.

And the crowd eye, what would the poor thing do then,
do then? Hungry for the stupid murders, the foolish law,
the sting of sin. Punch considers his threat, his opportunity,
his poetry.

Punch Runs into Another Daydream

This is not the same beast in crooked nights,
faces crawling on the collapse of reason, screams with their
treason and torn robes, always the bells heaving the ringers off the
ground like the executed dead.

This is rock and snow day and the soldier with death
in his song, a window with a dozen views, winds that come
from sardine cans, the rain
in a rat's warm eyes.

Punch hovers in his box with the man nearby.
Punch lies down in his neat suit of lies.

Punch Asks His Questions

'Who's a pretty baby then? Who's a pretty baby then?
What a pretty baby. What a lovely day.
WHO IS THE GOD?
What a lovely weapon then. What a lovely bomb then.
What a lovely wound. Who's got a lovely bomb then?
WHO IS THE GOD?
What about a funny song? What about a funny song?
Here we go; one, two, three. We all love the sea.
Three, four, five. Is the snowman alive? Four, five, six.
Who is the god? What a lovely god, then. What a
pretty god, then. Give the god to mummy then.
Ask the judge to hold the god. Help. Help.He's
dropped the god. Where he gone?'

Punch Disappears

The mirror fails again. There has to be more
than images.

Punch moves his right arm and sees the
right arm raised.

This is not enough. There have to be
miracles somewhere.

Punch winks his left eye and sees the
left eye wink back.

He moves his mind slightly; just so.
He has never doubted so much before.

Punch rushes at the mirror
and keeps on going.

Escape.

Looking back, he raises the right
arm again; and nothing happens.

This must be death.
He grins.

from *Return to the Abode of Love*

Return to the Abode of Love

I
Beneath these English trees
the world's messiah spoke of love.
Outside the village tongues
rattled reason, strung-out the lie.
The coach that rode from Bridgwater
bore the lamb of God.

Each week he prayed with them
took their love and wealth, trading
dreams to choose his seven maids
(one for each night) and the real God
let him survive. *But what in his room*
after the flesh did his own soul say?

II

In the chapel the silver plaque
still marks the grave of this messiah.
Buried upright, the purple glass permits
its days of fragile light and silence.
The village organist arrives with the rectory boy
to pump his magic into rigid air.
The prints of bathing women and woodland
scenes hang in huge frames like ghost-dream
images. *There's nothing real surrounding us.*
The moment is mosaic and clutches for
some meaning. *There is no cure.* The chapel
falls in time and nothing will regain reality
where God was cheated. The upright dummy Christ
kicks in his silent flames or screams for eternity.
There is no joke beyond this trick. God roars 'imposter'
in the plug of dust that was once an actor's brain.

III

One mile away the church clock
tells the almshouse villagers
to leave their gardens, to wake, to eat,
to prepare for ordinary events.
The stone tower has a pink stone
quiet as the roses in their gardens.
They remember stories of the Christ.
They recall the tales. They have
no notion of the injury to their
ordinary God, his ancient trust.
Their village has not entertained
the real Christ. *The cedar trees
move slowly in the summer wind.*
In winter the snow returns.

from *Replies for My Quaker Ancestors*

Knock Knock

Four Poems   For W.S. Graham

1

Why are you reading this?
A mind within its rattle,
reason roaring into words,
the yelp of self
searching for truth's
ragged fiction
neatly caressing the
flesh of reason.

Why are you reading this?
Coming into understanding
and not understanding.
Surviving the search for
meaning with your own
beings. The voice leads
to another voice. The
doubt dresses in its bones.

Why are you reading this?
Letting it read you. It
encounters your hours, your
lives, your careful festivity.
You hear your own dream-drone,
epistles and texts, clatter, clatter.
Is it you or your wound
that turns over the page?

2

And when you go into your sleep
that is not words but saying,
do you also take me with your
images and years, do we two
and the girls enter old Indiana
or the revolutionary coffee party,
do we also sit in a plane
that has no wings?

And when you go into your sleep
that is not living but being,
can my gift of likening, can
our family of understanding,
fight with the rages, the words
that flame, the water that will
not be silent, the pebble
slowly stopping up your throat?

And when you go into your sleep
is it because you know I am here
inside the years, inside the silence,
inside the clockwork shadow,
that you do not die in dreams,
crack bones and burn in terror,
rage beyond my love that is
a light to waken you?

3

What will you do
when you have hidden yourself
in other words, official histories
other afternoons?

What will you do
when the numbers do not
add up to rainbows;
the figure one dissolves,
the figure two escapes,
the figure three
is never here?

What will you do
when the mirror is night,
when your children tell you
that Belsen is a food,
when the book says that
poetry is a bone,
when the poem tells you
that to start
is to end?

4

I hear the words rattle
and I wait for
my very own silence.

In a place like Madron
the distance is always
the quarrel of
winds and land.

The mirror gives back nothing.
The biro mutters.
Between two days
what we must always
call night
descends.

I am reminded
of the dreams.
They do not get
out of the lift.
They do not leave
the quiet room.

I cannot write about
them. I cannot not write.
I cannot be with them or
within them.

Pass me some words, again.

Replies for My Quaker Ancestors

1

Returning in summer to the rectory in Somerset
the words are there, still there:
'not now, not now.'
How can that garden, that building, enclose such coils,
codes, circumstance?
Years of rain, storm, snow and sun
seem to have washed round them:
'not now, not now.'

Not that such words were ever spoken, hang
here as tokens within me. And I bring them
back, I return and feel their centres.
Ghost of my father hurrying to the church
beneath a cedar tree. Ghost of an old lady
who sat by my side as I learnt to drive
round and round the rectory drive:
'not now, not now.'

And standing here, memory within memory,
and now writing this down, and you reading this,
what are we doing with these words,
these sentences in our lives,
these beings within shadows
that we sense are the beginnings of other things?
All my life, all my words, all our worlds:
'not now, not now.'

2

When the words did not come,
where did the words go, gather?
In the silence that is bone-time
the talk that cannot utter
did not (does not) cease its rattle,
roar, releases. Where am I in this?
Do the words wait, want intervals,
retreat? Is there some store I do not
seem to know but seem to sense?
When the words are away
what alarms them, returns them,
recalls what I think they should
be about being about in me?
What words do I use for these words?
What is the precise body
of this silence shrieking?

3

Sometime I have no wish to
take this any further. It would
seem best to rest at this table
and stare at some pebbles or
dream of no more letters or repeat
a single sentence over and over
until it is indeed over.
But the scurrying will not cease.
The attractions are still there.
The faces roar. The snow day

intrigues because of its impulse.
Even the snow day. Even the silent.
Even the not looking very hard, the
trying to get on with something else.
What is this nonsense that I seek
between other things? What is this
disturbing prick without it?
The day hangs back. The history
of the hour jabs at meaning.
The conquest of intervals does
nothing to assist. Even the snow
as it falls, falls down onto everything
covers nothing, provides a change.
I look again and see it changed.
I begin again.

4

'And why are you so long at the words,
making them yours, owning ideas,
your sentences; what are they
set against?'
In the Quaker meetings content without
the noises of words, the worry and rattle,
uttering, muttering.
Just let them move within their snows.
In the Quaker house the God
or sense of God behind the waiting,
behind the faces behind the hands,
behind the memory of love and age,
the rumour of regret, the voice
that is not words.
What am I doing with the words
in this particular respect?

5

In the old letters, what we may now call
the dead letters, the finished sentences,
there is a conversation that we have
made, and survived, and changed.
In the old family diaries that used to
clutter, mutter, rattle in my father's
untidy study, his little ruin, his
office of old voices and dead whispers.
He needed it all there. He needed them.
In the old letters, what we may now call
dead conversation and conversion
so that the voices and conversion
are still there. Listen to them; listen.

6

As this is written it is written
between a sense of order, of record,
and poetry and dream. It is my
dream and the words are dreaming.
It is lonely and shared.
It is mutter and mosaic.
And you, reading this; what do
you say. Now, what do you say?
Howl it down, rage it to ruins?
Laugh it into poor, trite litter?
The litter of love, the drizzle of
dreams! What have you said?
'Not now, not now.' But what
time will there ever be for you
to receive this as more than tokens,
heart-tasks, ghost replies?
What have you also been doing
with the words and the time
for words and the times without words?
Who are you in my words?
Who are you in your own words?
'Not now, not now.' The never-never

decision, the never-never roar, the
life leaping these intervals so that
the words never catch you out,
catch you in, catch you at all.
Now, say it: what do you say
and whose words are you living in?
A pause. Begin again. Say.

Six Poems for My Father

1   Sometimes I See My Father

Sometimes I see my father in the tallest nights
struggling with his identity of love,
certain of absolutely everything as he harshly hums
through hymns that I have heard him butcher
since I was five.

One day he caught me
there in the bedroom in front of the Victorian mirror,
lipstick on each cheek, my shirt reversed, rehearsing my sermon,
God's Russian clown.

Once in Turkey we stood in a holy place
poor women whispering pain and old men crying close to
the sacred ground; my father was not sure what we should do
and so he smiled at me and stood at attention,
clenching my hand.

When grandfather died he tied the sun in knots
getting us all in place, in uniform, the right approach
to a grief I could not feel with my bowler hat and the taxi
breaking down and great-uncle catching his hand in a prayer.

Finally my father found his God, the hiding place was revealed.
His flesh was fire in Devon, his ash was rock in Cornwall.
Now his books surround me,
his stares sit down;
his words play with the girls out on the autumn lawn.

2 *My Father Talking of God*

My father, talking of God, walking on the vicarage lawns, past
the sunken tennis court, the ancient elms, the path that
led to the centre of a ruined hedge, our secret camp.
He always amazed me. His 'hot line' worked. He spoke
of desert miracles, stones that danced, the ever-ready
angels. He saw no problems. There were no rival gods.
There were no silences. The void was there because
the God was there. There at the deepest centre abode
a spirit we could not name. There at the edge of everything
hovered the God. The mind was light. The word was mirror.
My father, talking of God; a universe beginning with the letter A
never reaching the letter Z.

3 *Coming Forward Going Back*

Beneath the hidden lily pond
I hunt my father's missing stars.
This is where the tortoise died.
It dug too deep into its winter shield;
it did not know or sense that death and life
are inches in the gap of time.

And here we buried goldfish, wrapped in silver
paper, empty Players packets crammed with daisy
heads and stiff bent fish; each container named,
each grave-mound marked with a broken slate.

Once, my father's dog collar fixed with pins,
surplice blowing in an Easter wind, I led my sister
and three friends with comic books and bells and dead
leaf wreaths down the graveyard path towards the door.
'O God, our help in ages past' we sang;

then ran like mad. The door had opened just before
our noise could coil towards the real coffin
carried by six men with hands like fish, gripping
some body in its helpless carrier bag.

Twenty years on I stand at this place.
The pond has disappeared. The roses are new.
I try to forget what we did to worms before
we buried them. The lawn is lettuce plants;
the vicarage is flats. Where the deck chairs stood I
halt; slowly I lower some words to the earth.

4 *Not My Father*

Not my father but the five men
who came before dusk with quiet suits,
who waited for a while in the drive
for my mother to say
goodbye and goodbye.

Not my father as I wait outside the room
and they zip him up inside their yellow bag;
slowly I lead them down
and down
and the front door is closed.

Not my father but a certain procession of words
and suddenly these marriages, these discussions
with gods;
each one of us has these arrangements
as we say goodbye, goodbye.

Not my father but flowers and music
and his choice of words;
evenings in his rooms,
hours with old ideas,
and the moon rattles, rattles.

Not my father but selling the house,
moving some of the garden plants.
One year later we still make these
attentions,
we are still so busy
saying goodbye and goodbye.

5   *After a Burial*

After a burial of things
we are united in
disorder;
          then,
once again,
someone starts
                to talk:
it is as if
you
had left some
                sentences
in
these
rooms.

6   *The Trees Grow Out for the Light*

The trees grow out for the light;
it is that certain.
And we are left without your words,
your robes, those
oh so formal rituals of fire and mind.

A raincoat that you seldom wore
remained for months;
stiff and bound in web and flies
it hung in folds like an ancient wave
or impossible bird.

We sold your car. The roses
that you refused to prune grew so tall,
the blooms were shaped like field mice
and died too soon.

We carefully stacked the diaries in
one place, and letters from the dead;
your four desks slowly leaked
old truths!

One year later, two, three, four;
your books are minds, the pictures hang again.
My study leaps and jumps in space.
I do not quite inherit things.

It is as if you had left some wounds.

Killing the Geese

He races round and round with blood
on his gut, stumbling after a single goose
that has broken its wing.

I have seen him killing a small bird
caught in the strawberry netting in June,
and in winter he helped the old pig
onto its feet
in a tide of mud.

Now he is killing. Between the trees that seem to
step aside, he grabs and grasps and
finally succeeds.

The long neck is placed beneath a pole,
the legs are pulled up; something snaps
and the body quickly freezes.

All day we have been doing this
and I carry the bodies of dead geese
in a wheelbarrow, then hang them
up from the legs.

Hanging from hooks in an outhouse
they dip and dive in their dozens
in the dripping cold light,
blood slowly leaking from
their beaks.

Five women, hired from the village each year,
pluck them as fast as they can.
Their fingers move like yellow ferrets
eating the feathers away.

Late at night I close the door.
Sixty geese hang like midget priests
after some terrible rebellion.

And the snow comes, comes down,
comes slowly down, all night
comes down.

In the Old England

Everything as an achievement
wallowing in the generous plague of existence:
seventeenth and eighteenth century picnic parties
sprawling over an English universe beneath everlasting
russet sun, stitched cloud and fresh oak, sharp smell of red
apple, stinging odour of boys with hoops, girls gathering giant flowers,
randy uncles simmering beneath sudden snores, extraordinary bull-huge

faces of grandfathers, pear-noses pickled with pox.
The greatest miracle was that they arrived there; jerked out from webby
mansions, down along dirt roads, coaches breaking down, wheels
     spinning off,
servants cheating and stealing: the inevitable fellow traveller, Mister death.
Everything as an achievement; and the greatest of these was that there was
ever time to do anything at all out of the ordinary, yet
they sought diversion with saintly enthusiasim
falling headlong between summer and autumn, dreading winter,
plunged between highwaymen and ragged priests,
stuffed pigs and savage cockerels,
black bell booms and
broken white fences.

Owl Poems

1

Owls enter the heads of the dead
as the sea cracks its seasons;
words itch across the dried up grasses.
It is Easter and owls who remember the slain Christ
curl up their resurrection dialogues,
performing again dark miracles
that only the sad and mad
might understand.
Owls observe the waves initiating their
own decay, lodging their bodies in the damage
of the famous dead
who wait for bells and the moaning procession of fears.
Owls count the trees holding out against snow,
hear sea ache, rock tick.
Their eyes shade rain,
their bodies gleam like the vomit of dead saints.
In their blood there are cold rivers.
In their blood there are damaged hymns.
In their blood there are dead children
running after owls.

2

When Dylan Thomas died an owl
flew through the hospital
and lay very close to his hurt brain.
This owl had a hairy song
and slow-motion pain
and a dream like a broken bottle.
It spun in the dark quiet,
it took the scream and hid it,
it climbed into an old man's shirt
singing of Wales in an American storm.
The poet, already dead, saw the shirt,
and thought that it was his own Welsh shirt,
and carefully dragged it over his head
with the buttons popping.
He put on the shirt with the owl inside
and the wind and the dream
and it felt very good.

3

When the words do not come
I think of the owl that comes
with its nights dragged like an
ancient worry behind it.
The owl keeps the moon inside
a rusty tin and waits for the moment
of poetic ruin; and jumps in the tin
marked 'solitary dreams'.
It says 'not now', and 'seldom',
and 'never'.
I hear the stones of its mind
bang and rattle.
When the words do not come
the owl pulls faces in the mirror,
picks at the silence, tugs at
my very own ruin.
It knows nothing
and plays with the holes in my brain.

The English Who Are Slightly Mad

The English, who are slightly mad in summer,
understand God's rain-territory, snow sermon,
fog night and fabulous thunder.

Summer forces them into precise gardens, green
and placid domains where earth is accounted a virtue
between cucumber sandwiches and small cups of tea.

So long as the tie or the braces do not have to be removed
all is pretty fair with home-made wine and decorated drives
and wives who bend gently like trained winds.

Lawns are for walking around, trees are for carefully
contrived meetings which must never take place;
the sun is always quite perfect
when setting.

All summer we wonder how Constable achieved it;
not a drop of dust, grass as an art, and dogs
that don't pant.

At night we play Mozart, small glasses are passed round,
our heavy bedrooms roll slightly until three o'clock, a gentleman's
snores are short and warm.

Every day we find things for other people to do; cricket
to stimulate the sinews, croquet slow enough for the cameras,
tennis for the energetic or the mad.

Rigging up a deck chair is designed to take an hour or two.
Only the very old should consider bathing in the nude.

All summer we wait for the autumn.
It is an ideal death.

In the Three P.M. Room

1

Lying down on the couch, lying
down in the three p.m. room, lying
down between the pictures and wallpaper
and small tables with journals,
I can see the doctor's eyes riding
above his spectacles, riding above
two ugly mobiles, riding on his face
of serious pink meat.

2

The memory will do it all for me,
lying down to explore days, to endorse
ways, to expose myself between
pictures and wallpaper and journals
and tables that are so tidy, so steady,
so necessary. The voice is all there is,
there is this noise of voice from the doctor
and then my own noise. The tables have
gone, the journals are never read. The
necessary voice is like an empty vase.
The glass reveals a growth of dust,
even here.

3

I can see my mother folding a tablecloth.
She does this most carefully, gently. Everything
in her being is concentrated on this necessary act
of folding across, over, across, over. It is silent.
The table beneath the cloth is silent. There are
some journals on a table and they also are silent.
I can see her working with the tablecloth. It is white
and made of strips from a parachute. It is
a war time tablecloth and it is 1940 and
I am unborn. Then the doctor enters the room

and shows her photographs of bombing raids.
They both turn to smile at me. The doctor
offers me a journal.

4

The doctor is barking again. He should not
be doing this. Either I am paying him too little
or his wife earns too much or he is getting too many
ideas from the journals. I must check up on him.
Perhaps he is a little mad today. Perhaps the dust
is composed of history, composed of compressed ruins,
so that the future and past mingle on the glass.

5

What I want to say is being recorded
in this small room. Small compressed history
lies in ruins around the journals and we will call
this dust. It is also life. Because I have no money
I will pay the doctor with photographs. I have a nice one
here. My mother is laying a table for a meal.
The photographs show her quite clearly. She has removed
certain journals from the table and now she lays a
white tablecloth to conceal the wood. Nobody is
expected to eat off the wood. Nobody is expected
to eat on a dusty table after all. Nobody is
going to stand (or sit) for anything but a fine
and tidy meal. The photograph shows all of these
details and not a speck of dust. What I am saying
is being recorded with great dexterity by a
beautiful machine. The room is made up of
small strips of reality and in some places
there are particles of memory: shall we call
it dust?

The Dry God

In Memory of John Berryman in his blue chair

I am going to talk of the dry god.
It is not the comfortable, encouraging, hallelujah god.
It is not the climb into my wisdom, my dazzle, holy father of flowers
and mountains god. It is not the ancient grammar god.
It is not the hidden within such silence is my meaning, I am this
and that, hold firm to the remnants of my visions god.

The dry god comes in the terrible long nights,
howling from the locked rage, heaving from the deeps,
arching monster mumble, muttering breaking mosaic,
crying time into sad sand.

Plantations crack. Sun skins the eyes of the young.
The old men creak into shadows of castles.
The dry god stuffs dead grass into the minds
of the poets. Wind sucks the river dead.

The dry god pushes a man out to be a prophet
when all they want is wind and dance.
The dry god says 'go on, be a prophet'
and the whole town hisses.
The dry god pushes a new symphony into the dead
composer's funeral flames, screams vows in the
ears of the mad, mutters moral equations
at the whore house doors.

Sometimes the dry god observes the other god,
sees the tricks, never misses a miracle,
hears hermit prayers, eternal chant
and rant, rant, rant.

The dry god visits ruin upon ruin upon ruin.
He creaks where the cross stood. He coughs
where old ladies have cried. Sometimes
he tells himself a blue joke
where a vision took
its place.

Oh do not call this dry god the devil.
Do not say the dry god is no god.
Do not deny that the God
has no doubts.

Across the surface of time there are millions
of cracks, scrawls, smutty messages.
Between the storms and silences the
mutters mean.
Between a planet's destruction and the
birth of grass
God's doubt hanging like a bloody owl.

The dry god cannot stop laughing.
He feels the huge bruise of faith buzzing.
He waits for the other god to send him
messages, apologies even, suggestions, texts.
He waits as each planet leaks. He plucks
power as some humans' petals.

Sir Edward Elgar Hang-Gliding over Worcestershire

It has to be late summer but not yet autumn.
We do not want the leaves doing 'poetic' things
and we do not want an air of expectancy
at the race course in Worcester.

God's vantage point; up and away in a wind
that tickles his spats, but nothing more than
that. We do not want surges of storms, doom
across the country Langland knew.

Elgar is fully operational; but this is nothing
more than we should expect of an English composer,
a man in this position gains certain things.
From such a height he cannot even hear the fair
ground music. He can only just see Malvern Wells
and the road to the motorway and his very own
grave.

If Shaw gets to hear about this he will no doubt
tremble in his bubble bath. If the publicity boys
get into it the sky will be crowded with wings.
If he discovers God up there the festival
will be ruined.

It is now about three-thiry and possibly time
to prepare the tea.

from *A Banquet for Rousseau*

Warnings in Advent

Listen; their words are filling the dark corners.
They bring out old hymns like friendly flags.
Between stones built once for other gods
they kindle grace against a howling season.

Look; the very old have the faces of children,
it is the ancient who settle things in the dark.
A child is laid down with rose buds in its mouth.
The villages are stranded in oceans of snow.

Hear us in these words we give you; oh do not
let them fall to dust. Keep the door ajar
in case a saint arrives.
Leave room at the table for love.

My Father's Ghosts

My father's ghosts did not come at night.
At his desk, hitting out at the typewriter
he wrote about Irish ancestors and believed
in them.

Names like 'Clogheen' and 'Cooleville'
captured him, and then he found the family in America
at Grubb's Landing, the Potomac and
Chesapeake Bay.

After six hours of writing
he watched soap operas and sometimes
read thrillers, but in reverse. He began at the
final chapter and worked backwards just to get
a new ring to normal things.

He gave up 'The Archers' for 'Crossroads' and never got into
'Coronation Street'. In retirement he ran a toy
shop and when he tired of that he started writing
'Grubbs About The Globe'.

It was hard talking to him. That last Sunday in July he stared out
at the overgrown garden sensing loss, trying to get me
to stay longer as if guilt were a trick he could
still deploy.

Mother rescued us.
He sat in a terrible dressing gown smiling at his own ideas,
working his way through a mound of newspapers
as if another world could be trapped within.

Each day he read old diaries and letters from
two generations back. He was drifting now, no
longer bossing, having his say in the obvious way.
But still he kept us in our place with questions,
curious asides, and that sad and hunted look.

Four days later I hurried back. His body sagged
in silence. I remember his final words.
He said he expected to live another twenty years
and planned a trip to Mexico.

The Deserted Church

It is not so easy now. This doubt cannot be met
with wine or words. The real world murders God,
it strikes down miracles and battle hymns hang
in the ancient flags like unholy ghosts.
Ice and fire rush out to greet the God who
fumbles planets, forgets his secrets, spits out wars.
Wings of shame hang in the trees of dreams.
Old stars scream mercy in deserted space.
Oh do not say we do not love the God. We made
him merciful, we gave him brilliant scenes and
reaped compassion from a field of stones; but now
this God believes in us, will not forget.

The Church in Summer

God's sun enters through thirteenth century glass.
It is an ancient warmth that comforts,
words moving into the memory of music.
Hands reach out for blessings. We bring
an ordinary world to the god and wait for miracles.
The old lean on hope and the very young are carried

towards a light that must last all of their lives.
This light is God's chant, his sun and moon
before the planet breathed. It is truth's doubt
and His grace in a terrible silence that must
enter our souls in the time when all of us have gone.
It is God's music when he is finally to be left alone.

The Church in Winter

Wind eats stone, yelps snow, hurts God's harsh
bargain against so many faiths.
Few people come here, love or doubt dragging them
back in small congregations
to make this music against oblivion.
The light through old glass seems to have drained
from forgotten seas. Is it God's laughter
we hear in this ruin of rain? Are these His tears?
A simple bell sounds out the loss of years;
a carol for Lazarus or Mozart,
snow crawling against the legends of graves again,
the clock tower telling us things we sense
but cannot believe.

Islands

What are these islands of the mind
that return, come again, will not let go?

There are no homes here, winds play yahoo
between trees stranded in blizzards.

There are no other visitors here, we meet ourselves
coming back, retreating, ready to begin again.

There is no strange beauty, an alphabet of doubt
disturbs contentment, muddles the map, masks the plan.

Angles of light keep us moving, desiring, designing
another place. The dark bell of reason hangs silent.

What are we making here? What wound of truth
lies hidden beneath the track of words?

Between trees dead days hang like spies. They
have failed, they have forgotten. They have no homes.

Jesus in Hell

Day One

Am a Judas claw. Am a Gethsemane time clock.
Am a cock with a human eye. Am a bell with a mind.
Am an old mouth stuffed with stones.
Shaped into a curse, my tongue a wire, I speak glass.
There is no moment I can secure, no silence I can gain.
Twelve men laugh at me.
A woman called Mary screams at me as her long hair burns.

Day Two

I am sitting in the boat again. My friends are talking
about what it was like in the old days. They seem to want
to return to those days. None of them looks at me. They dare
not. It is as if I were a ghost already. Suddenly the sea is
filled with fish. Each fish has the eyes of a young child as
the bodies heave and jump about on the deck.

Day Three

The master of this place wants me to agree with him.
He has been around a long time. He wants to share things.
Certain of his schemes he thinks I might approve of. For
example; a great deal could be done about war. He shows

me some of his plans. Life will get better for millions. The
idea of joy will become all important. Men will help each
other. Things will begin to run so smoothly there won't be
any need for a god. Entire nations lie down to sleep.

Voices

How to get the voice right
speaking to oneself of others, or by oneself
rehearsing in preparations, in proposals.
So to speak, not too near to consience, the
consequences of vocabulary and grammar and tradition.
I do not favour disbelief but it's a good beginning point,
it is where the blood and intellect wrestle, jump up
to fight. Ah yes, the intention to be brave as well as
eloquent, to make a go of it, to publish one's proposals
and let there be a response. The clearing of throats. The
crafted replies. 'This writer creates new worlds... The poet
opens gates... The beautiful fictions of truth...' etc, etc.
So to begin, each time to begin, as if a miracle might open
its glories and remain in the blood and pass through words
to 'open' worlds, to bring down the light from mountains.
And so here we are again, you have come to listen, or to see
me trying out my brave new words, and I enter your heads;
and am changed, my disbelief becomes certain, my caution
becomes a flag, my attempt is recognized as an achievement
of some sort. It is a finished thing. And if there is applause,
the next poem is already being prepared for, the silence is
too long, dreadful. I even suggest reading the same poem
again and again until it is fully mine, yours, ours, the
real poem. At best you sense me, you like or dislike
or I fail you. The page turns. The poem is over. When
it is read again, by you, by me, it cannot be the same.
It is like the extraordinary flight of wild geese, that
sound of wings, that break of light and furnished sky.
The sky is light, is not ours, kindles.

from *A Romanian Round*

A Romanian Round

there are no toys so they do
not play   if they do not play
there are no images   if there are no
images there are no words   if there are
no words there are no expressions   if there are
no expressions there are no other worlds   if there
are no other worlds there are no symbols   if there are
no symbols there are no journeys   if there are no journeys
there are no dreams   if there are no dreams there are no celebra-
tions   if there are no celebrations there are no memories   if
there are no memories there is no history   if there is no
history there are no events   if there are no events
there is no identity   if there is no identity
there is no proof   if there is no proof
there is no existence   if there is no
existence there are no toys
there are no toys

The Romania Tree

Does not hold birds.   Does not let light
    enter.   Keeps out stars and sunsets.
Spies out the land.   Holds close thousands of dreads,
    clutches secrets.   Soldiers sleep beneath it.
In summer it listens, twitches with recording devices,
    plots the activities of farmers and priests.
It loves winter.   Pain is frozen in every limb.
    Its boughs tap out signals of atrocities.
And in spring; ah, in spring it is most terrible of
    all.   It sends out messages of renewal
as if oxygen was a trick, each leaf a policeman,

102

the earth itself designed to deceive.
Scuttling beneath its lowest branches the rats
    wait for abandoned babies.   And the bells from
the distant city remind the tree of massive forests.

from *The Rain Children*

In Shining Night

In these gardens, these declarations, these codes
I see my mother carefully collecting the large lilies,
sacred flowers, fragments of dance, the huge stamen
like an improbable tongue within the ghost demise; the measure
always of silence, of peace, of coiled respect, of naiveté.
And my father fumbling his favourite fictions still, the fag
sticking to his lips to seize the stammer, to halt despair,
always denying his doubt, always forging new adventures, fresh
etiquette; the bells of reason so ordinary, so cheap, so cold.
And now, you're gone, run out, surpassed, I admire what I despised,
I made famous and fabulous. The order re-ordered. The anger collapsed
into a stained glass window. I see the boy in the vicarage garden
with his uncertain smile, his stooped dreams, his secret pledge. And it is
always the large houses that collect, beckon, token;
the ancient trees and autumn lawns and rejected beacons of church bells.
The terror of reality. The hunched shadows of truth. The clamour
of doubt. The rooms in huge houses crowded with adults content
to cry. The old bandaging their ruins in cadenzas of creed.
The caw caw of the rooks reeling in circles of jeaopardy,
the progress of dreams stretching in the clouds of dawn,
the wild grass of Cornish cliffs turning on wheat white tides.
In shining night the carol of stars.

Another Energy

What would you have us do now? Gather in
all the achievements of faith and come to your funeral
with nothing but conviction, my sister so distresssed,
my wife and daughters catching hold of your summer days
when afternoon tea was a feast and you waved us farewell
across the ragged rose beds, the garden warning us?
Friends came from Somerset and after the service we
recalled your energy, your loyalty, your determination
to smile and always find the light. And now, four months
later, we are ready to bury the ashes, the small urn,
in Cornwall where all the childhood memories began.
Will it be a sea wind wail again, the gulls bobbing
like lost kites, or the blue grey sea music, the
rooks rocking the tall trees, the same ancient land
and earth struggling to recreate, stone walls packed deep
in another energy? And what would you have us do now,
preparing for this final ceremony, this necessary
departure, this saying farewell again,
when you've been so much with us, even closer now,
simply changing your meaning to our lives?

Mother, Stooping in the Early Light
For Sara

Mother, stooping in the early light,
inspecting the lilies, their cold flames, their silences.
She adjusts the complicated heating mechanism and the oil heaters
in the immense conservatory with tiled floor and wrought iron
decorations. She is an expert at this. Each year she is
bringing them on or holding them back to be ready
for Easter morning. From this protected territory they
will be gently carried in baskets and slowly driven to
the neighbouring churches. Each one has kept a week
of holy silence, the dark shades of contemplation

holding a dense glow. But she must be ahead
of all this, making ready for these flags of success,
their glow held in a single flame of adoration,
to remind us of a survival, the resurrection trick,
the flowers in the early light now responding
to her skills, her respect; each one like a
novice; a young woman preparing for a dance;
a bloom that will radiate what our words
cannot quite express. And my mother stands
there now, her delivery list carefully confirmed,
each lily fragile as ancient glass, waiting
for the light to rise and rise, unfurling the
fertility of faith.

Going Out

Mother, going out with her carols, her small tones,
her song that took over the words, consumed all meaning;
finally her hands quite still, each finger finishing its energy,
so that in my arms I held a head simply, the soft soft
going out, releasing this meaning;
and we were left with essential, practical details;
prayers and songs and some other person's words of comfort.

Alone

She would like there to be someone
there to share the start of this day.
her single spoon and knife settle by
the bowl, the cup and saucer, the side
plate, the napkin ring she insists upon.
And she will sit here, alone, the day
commencing, the morning ready to go,
the gulls in the bay screwing sounds

from the other side, the other reality.
She sits, consumes, sticks to this
ritual, this essential trick of
conformity. The beginning to each
day smells of tea and toast and on
Sundays a hard boiled egg. And
even the second chair, always there,
at the side of her, as if some day
there will be a guest, a visitor. She
has it placed there, always there.
She would like to share the start
of this day. She would like to speak
of it to somebody other than the radio
person, the newspaper voice, the whisper
of her dress and other things. She sees
sometimes how the bones of her fingers
and the handle of her knife have grown
alike. Ivory. Paled with age. Once
beautiful. She would like there to be
someone there, to be there, to be here.

Always Burying My Father

Always burying my father, who will not lie down,
the words clinging to the bone of dream, the short fictions of hope;
who is it who enters the door each day, smiles and frowns,
the festivity of remembering, the essential soliloquies of no?

It is easier to greet him now, distance reduces us all,
and even his eccentric dress can be a pleasure; the boom becomes
a song and where we stumbled is saved by a joke, a call
to retreat, an agreement to disagree at hates and loves.

And now it is too late to tell him I forgive, seated
at his desk, his pipe rack neatly placed between the books,
one drawer still locked, the key lost, as if small secrets
were waiting there; an image of winter in his summer truths.

Ghosts

I am waiting for my father's ghost
to arrive across the crowded room and shout
I am sorry. I love you.

I am waiting for his ghost to put down the terrible
cigarette butt, the Bible bulging with silences, and say
I agree. I am sorry. I am with you.

I am waiting in the field of sea music, the forest of rags,
the glade of drums, for his ghost to arrive in Wagnerian
propensities, to leap from the light that belches from crevices
to proclaim peace, acceptance, arrival, No Smoking.

Meanwhile words still gather in huge rooms, mirrors dance
gently together; I grow older and the wisdom slips down
between library silences, images of cold stone, windows
looking out onto abandoned tennis courts.

The Blue Chair
For Clare & Emily

I

The fiction of fact and one's deliverance from it
so that from the blue chair one is able to come across
recollections and recognitions and still see the distance
as new, discovery, fable, acceptable. And always the
comfort of voices, stories, anecdotes, the poetry of reconciliation;
the postcard of one's life perched in an obvious place as if we were
about to let loose in mad balloons, sail above certainty, or
build wings of disdain; or having written thin postscripts we
close the door, take a black and white train, a sepia journey
to the ice lands, the distant cold, to let the fear freeze
on the page in the ice-capped mind. The need for such escapes
as one seeks deliverance. The need of knowledge when all the time

the diary declares who we really are, the letter posted in our mind
screams betrayal, the song cannot be sung, the dance would
break our legs. And so it is this thing, this huge thought,
that catches us yet again between the sea path that calls
and the dream we cannot totally recall and still the dictation of
desires. The ordinary door. The simple window glass. The blue
chair in the sun or in the rain. A sudden image of boys
racing into the centre of the field in the midst of a thunderstorm;
braced into bravery, hurling caution, demanding courage.
In the centre of the field willing each one of us to stand still
and stare at the evening green sky, the tall terror of it,
the hurtling rags of it, the brawling beasts of it,
the ripped skins of drums and warrior flags and bandit rage,
the tribal ruin of it; waiting for it to fall, to fall,
to discover us there, to consume our status and souls.

II

And it is this ordinary door that opens to other rooms
where our lives collide or collect in hallways of memory as the sea
gently washes against the grandfather clock, the waves lap a
green tea trolley, my grandmother falls out of her heaped bed
and tennis rackets float out of the bay like biscuit-thin banjos.
And I see my mother again in the rose garden, her white hair filled
with moths, her mind muddled in a psalm of petals and apple
blossoms and calm orchards of Somerset. My father again chasing
the Chinese geese into the small barn, his mind dazzled with
carols and Irish ancestors, the church clock striking bats
and doves, gulls strutting on his typewriter in the study
strewn with family charts, Quaker diaries, the creak of country
houses, sermons scratching their solemnities across his dreams.
And lost in a tree house, in an air balloon, in a space rocket,
in a stage coach, racing between cedar boughs and the
scream of vultures, I meet again the boy hiding from Latin
declensions, the tricks of arithmetic, the appalling thuggery
of physics, the declarations of blank pages. And the drive
to the vicarage again fills with the faces of the dead. And
the small bedroom cupboard heaves with beasts. And the
curtains if they were to be drawn back would reveal the

curses of Custer and Captain Ahab and the eagle eyes
of Geronimo, the bowed down compulsion of Captain Scott.
Snow climbs onto the bed end. Sea runs beneath
the door. Ice enters the tuck box.

III

Sitting again in the blue chair, the garden slipping into evening
and the tulip fires now cooling, one is again aware of the blackbird's
warning signal. Is it the cat prowling along the garden wall or the
woman next door banging away at the telephone or perhaps the green
umbrella gently flaying away as if it has just remembered the thrill of
flight? And we are lifted up, rise above this gentle scene, the
commuters racing to the car park and the secretaries with clicking heels
not seeing us as we float above the roof tops now heading for
the hills. The blackbird falls silent. The houses disappear. Even
the church tower and the tallest trees vanish as we enter a cloud
of sublime silence. The green umbrella and the garden table and chairs
have risen with us. The wine glasses and the Sunday newspapers
and my wife's sunglasses remain fixed to the table and the cloud
carries us higher until the light filters to stars and a nearby
aircraft passes us like a silver pencil, totally silent. And
the blue chair itself has become silver in this flight.
Its sturdy frame assures me that this is not a dream. The
cloud departs and we are left in the arc of a mystery. The
trick is never to question, to sip some more wine, to ignore
the newspaper which belongs to another reality, the umbrella
also. We can remain here for hours. We can count
the stars and wait for the sun to come up from somewhere.
We can accept all this, believing all the time in the
certainty of the silver light and the sound of the wings
that are always near, gently moving with us, gently
growing larger and larger until all we can sense is this
power of flight, this space to travel, this precision.

Priest

I.

And when each one of them had left
after the convivial shuffling of pleasantries,
only a few with any words of real meaning
and those who could never look him in the mind,
he always remained in the church awhile,
silent within the heaped prayers as if they
also waited before entering the coil of their commission,
perhaps filtering between the fears and ambitions and
what was fact rather than loose frames of fiction.
It was as if the seconds between the ending of some
major work of music and the massive din of applause
were delayed, as if something else were to come,
as if the God would not so easily accept this
incantation of desires, the ritual and respect
had to fall away to reveal what meaning meant.

II

And at times this was indeed the only time
that he could enter the silence that he longed for,
when nothing was expected of him, when his own words
could pitch behind what others made of them, the
haul of duty and liturgy, each prayer and text loaded
with expectation, coils of custom and convention, so
that each second was plundered by necessity, what could
be easily identified and consumed smothering the pause
to doubt, to wrench out a new meaning, to compel
the soul onwards as if there were only this radiant path.
Then this silence, this great escape, as if he had the power
to dismantle it all, to dismiss every bit of it, to
stand up now and say this was no more than passionate
muttering, not the belief but the confusion of faith,
not the statement but the dream of its need.

III

It was mostly the seasons that called them back,
even the saddest squires at Christmas, and at Easter
farmers who had given up their fear of God yet haunted
by the bark of bells, the green man skipping into their dreams,
the tall ghosts of elemental trysts. And when they were not
here to name or claim they lifted their dead with flowers,
the young men trussed into borrowed suits, the women watching
their children disappear, and a few chewing anger beneath
the bitter text of time, the determination welling in their
minds to hate this God, to dig this land until its blood
were oil or gold, to hack back meaning and carve identity
out from the filth of barns, the reek of sheds, the cold
call of the February field. Some of these men would only
return here once. Some closed doors on reason. A few
heard words like tigers, strode out with flames in their minds.

IV

Sometimes he lacked what simple exchange was necessary. It was
easier to listen to the women or children. There was a
shadow in the minds of the younger men, some trick of discipline
or disorder so that it was necessary to stick to the
comfortable, the well-observed; they dreaded the stench of
mystery. Or was it history; did they see him coming out of
the village school, a threat to their freedom; was he
woven into the awkwardness of sterile sermons, the rasp of
orthodoxy, the dreaded cant of grey memorials and ornate
guilt cursed at by their fathers, ridiculed in the pub?
The lisp of eccentricity lingered in this rejection. The men
who pulled bells never stayed for the service. It was only
the older men, their huge hands gripping the
hymnal as if it might fly, their awkward singing,
waiting for a single truth, to bury it, to deep enfold.

V

In the silence of his room the words he would
say waited to become. His sermon always began
from the silence ready to be filled, the open notebook,

the discipline sharing his articulation; the words that
should have come from the meaning now coming as always
to meet him half way, to make a meaning, to give him
the voice that would seldom determine anything but self.
And cast upon the congregation, each mind capable of
self-definition, each life ready to re-order whatever he
said, the words and sentences and flourishes like some small food
that could be partaken quietly, each noise gently setting
down, each hymn slowly consumed, the heads and faces of
people he knew like strangers; no eyes to wink back trust,
no codes to urge him on. It would always be the same.
From the pews their own senses singing back a small song.

VI

Sometimes seeing the men come home from the fields,
farms, the heat of summer and the stubborn state of winter,
he wished for words that would seal some respect, of
recognition or encounter or defeat. It was not pride.
It was not the sting of satisfaction. It was cold and hard.
Observing Sam Frost at hedge laying he was again aware
of this. Each sapling cut down but not severed, saved to
fuse sap, to give out energy, the bill-hook perfectly shaped
to slice and stop, and finally lacing of another wood along
the top, the tap tap of his sideways axe, the security
of this craft handed on for generations; against wind and the
hurling rain and the defeat of reasons; against storm and doubt
and the self respect abandoned by machines and technology;
against the laws of progression and the fiscal logic and
the giving up of everything stained with blood and expertise.

VII

He gave them words and he gave the dead man grace.
As usual the dead man was traced by his anecdotes; his hobbies,
the hours in his garden, even his jokes; seldom a diary or a
letter; never a curse; and the secrets that may have been
between them were left in the litter of grief, of loss.
And with each comfort he gave them a chance to touch
things they had deserted for years, or had never known,

or had even made fun of. The church, the service, the grace,
or the cremation that seemed tidier if no easier in
the chaotic rocking of their minds. A place to make the
parting real, a ceremony of other people's words, the texts
to beat down the jungle of wrath. The essential considerations
and regulations. He gave them stories and songs to touch,
and held the candles of faith for them and in case they did
not dare light them, held out an ancient flame.

VIII

He stood again in the field of winter feeling the cold,
letting it lift him and wrap him and enter his doubt. It was
real, actual, something to be challenged, and yet welcome.
It told him of his foolishness, his idiotic penitence with
words and songs, the small successes that would all burn down,
finally be lost, inconsequential as each mind closed down to ice.
The doubt was strong as diamond, real in his stomach and soul;
and he wished to describe it in detail, totally recognise its
shape and power in this field of winter, this cold territory
of white sun and broken walls and ugly rusted abandonment.
He caught this doubt in his hands and lifted it up to
the great trees and the white sun and the pitching wind
and held it as high as he could; for the God and angels to
see, its stern attempt at power, its perfect pity.

IX

Between candle silence burning back on brass
and the light of stained glass clinging to 'amens',
this old confusion of meaning and its fictions, the need
to clarify and yet obedient to the context of mystery.
As if an idol were more certain than a dream, as if
the ending to each prayer were but prelude, as if belief
roared like a huge beast above the small creature of living.
Within the wine the essential concept of betrayal. Within
the bread the slightest fragrance of forgetting. Within the
hymn the road of sands in the desert places. And the wolf
roams beside the water where we would refresh ourselves, the lizard
creeps over the breasts of the naked women, the place

where a miracle has not yet taken its shape is visited
by wild dogs and bats. Between candles the whispers
of the words of the prayers you have not yet said.

X

And when each of them has assembled, ready now
for the roar of hallelujahs, the flames of lilies, the
bells to call them out of winter, the figures in the
Easter Garden to let them play again; when they are all
standing beneath this huge power to be above the
day to day, the light so immense now we are immersed
in praise, when all the palms have become trumpets,
what can he do then with his field of winter, his
pack of doubts, his vision of the blind man waiting to
see? He stands in the pulpit with his vocabulary of
charms, the games of prophets and seers in his bag,
the jack-in-the-box's Christ swaying on its spring,
and he hears his own voice and his father's voice and the
voice of the dead farmer and the voice of the youngest
child hurling down the silence, defeating it, excelling.

Stanley Spencer Arriving in Heaven
For Nick and Mary Parry

1

He is wondering if there might be trees;
and now he sees boughs
crooked and green greeting him.

He is wondering if there might be women;
and now he sees their arms, onion sheen
as they spread the celebration tables.

He is wondering if there might be words;
and now he hears angels gossiping.

2

It is silent. He opens his mind to a meadow of silence.
The light that falls on everything is the silver of springs,
the brown of deep held rocks, gold of fish kingdoms,
and the heron standing on the far bank
stares out at the splendour which
falls and falls until
the Lord of glory arrives
on His bicycle.

3

And the light that is falling
is held in the man's mind
as he deciphers his realities,
is deep set in the valley as the sun sets,
is driven in views of the village from a distance,
is present in the hurrying woman who again
makes her way to the chapel with a basket of lilies,
is held in the face of the infant in a large green pram.

4

Entering Heaven is to leap into such light
that Stanley Spencer has one face at two angles,
has one mind in green and one of snake silver, listens
to saints on one level and a small orchestra on another,
and then there is to be comprehended the saint
picking up his yellow umbrella in a field with a lion.

5

Spencer attends the roll call.
Spencer is asked to undress.
Spencer has his eyes looked at.
Spencer is asked to explain 'light'.
Spencer is given a chance to sing.
Spencer is left in an orchard of blossom
and told that he must wait.

6

At a distance so near it comes and goes
in the presence of the dark shrubs which are
all the time changing to gold.
Spencer watches what must be an angel
skinny dipping in what must be a lake.
At a nearness the dark gold body of the
angel who has taken off its wings to
protect an image of perfection. So near
coming and going the dark gold of the angel
who constantly dips beneath the water level
yet is never out of sight the deep water
somehow in sky or part of the air or part
of the body at a distance changing yet.

7

At intervals with himself Stanley Spencer
begins to dress himself in the clothes that
were left on the large blue table, the blue
having attracted him from the very first moment.
The blue it appeared had got into the clothes
so that the shirt and pullover and tie now hold the
blue. Even the wings he now struggled with
were part of this blue more than the white
he had expected, anticipated, accepted.
Now it was the blue, gradually the blue,
entirely the blue, all being the blue.

8

Assembled within the light lifting
ideas of the new. His mind not quite departed
and expecting to hold happy conversations with John Donne.
There are no steps to be scrubbed here and there is no difficulty
about departure. The light lifts ideas of the new and an
angel with a Gladstone bag may exceed Stanley's own steep
paradoxes. Ah; such parades, such poetry, such co-ordination.
He wonders now if this is Heaven. He wonders what will follow.
Stanley Spencer is not quite sure of this certainty, the angel with

the Gladstone bag; is he God or John Donne or Christ? Beneath
a bough of apples, Stanley seeks the real sky, the glorious
declaration beyond proof, the tight textures of certainties.
The way he might have come. The entrance he might have made.
The light lifting the scene, everything ascending; his total
awareness rising so that now all images integrate, abandon.
The sense of sense going. The self squeezed away. The light
absorbing his soul. The arching of it, the taking of it, the entire
exultation of light lifting Stanley Spencer into convictions.

The Rain Children

Always at a distance, as if this were the greatest trick,
whilst adults crowd to the tragedy or the miracle,
consumed in vast parades, bowed down by rituals;

they escape to the autumn beach, the cold boned
winter park, their voices now tokens driven past evergreens
and the stranded torsos of upturned benches;

and most of all I remember them in the gardens of
large houses, journeying into secret kingdoms, and once
in a Devonshire church a small silent boy

facing me back from a fragment of thirteenth century glass.

Uncertain Light

Is it the light entering
or the departure of a stream of silence
fused through this ancient glass,
this mosaic filter?

Are these hymns, these words pitched
into music, the meaning of truth
or the manner of what we would say
attempting these truths?

And who are we, being here to
declare these things, unable to
settle our doubts and beliefs alone,
collecting such trusts?

Oh we are here to be, to become,
always content to start out,
always happy to leap into
cascades of certainty.

It is only later, alone, huddled
within oneself, that the God or
doubt roars, rattles, fingers the
wound, will not let be.

from *The All Night Orchestra*

Lords and Prophets

LORD OF SHADOWS

We are remembered by our doubts. From
that distance I thought I saw a man
approaching on a horse, but when we drew closer
it was a dead tree; quite dead;
a tree. Nobody laughed. Nobody said
'I told you so, you tired old fool,'
although I know that some
considered that I was a little mad.
Then the women, in the garden later,
in the cool garden with light blue tables
and white deckchairs, said they had seen me

staring off into the distance at a long-dead tree.
They talked about this as if I could not hear. They
said I had a brilliant light in my eyes
and they feared what the morning's ride had done.
And I sat in a white deckchair aware that
the blue tables were very slowly moving
towards the sound of the sea. We are
remembered by our doubts, we are considered
as to our fears. We see moths in the eyes
of the old and hear the crab creak past
where there is no speech.

LORD OF DAWNS

In the beginning of each day, between the
determination to rise and live and continue, between
the cleaning of the body and eating and listening to other people's
news and the screaming clock and reading about yesterday,
there must always be a moment when death would seem preferable.
Each day millions must rush past this split-second loss of strength
and get out of their houses, into cars and trains and taxis, into streets
and roads and avenues, successfully escaping. Each day the impulse is
ignored, smothered, controlled. They leave and depart and become other
    selves.
The lord of dawns is aware of this. He can wait. A very select number
will not respond. They go from darkness into darkness. They die. They sleep
in. They enter their own specially prepared dreams. They hang themselves
on other people's fictions. They robe themselves in fantasies. And a smaller
number pray as they do it. They breathe in the new light and create
new meaning and dance a little as the postman delivers fresh
obstacles and challenges and impertinences.

PROPHET OF VOICES

Waiting again for the exact voice, the principle of thought, exertion
or intellect, the final declarations of genius in glass boxes, the total
abstract delivery; or not waiting. For it had not come in snowy fields,
in spring forests, on winter beaches, at deathbed soliloquies. He had called
in the apparatus of gigantic operas in small tents, into little rooms, waiting
for the diary to heave up and scream. He had so hoped for a revival of dreams.

Now came silence on its squat horse with picture postcards and long-distance phone calls and air letters telling him that the universe was OK. History was bouquets, literature a fine wine; the bank manager sent him Christmas cards. The young looked uglier, skinnier, chewing up the structures he had loved. The gristle of sex dangled between their legs caught by a grotesque lens. In carefully planted parks he saw his dream squeak like a rubber duck.

PROPHET OF SHADES

Where there is no speech I come to
create new dreams. You do this for me,
creating miracles, places of resurrection,
denials of death. In the small, miserable
houses there are always some people scribbling
away in diaries, poets of the junkyards, seers
in the storm. The fat architects of doom
dream up little fantasies for me to enshrine.
With the brains of dead men I make visions
that keep you afloat, visible, almost at
times contented. In a cool garden by the sea
an old man may stare at a blue table
and green striped deckchairs and remember
a desert journey years before; the experience
of a lifetime his wife calls it. He considers
that she is a little insane and pours cream
over the dome of a small silver spoon.

LORD OF BENDING LIGHT

I would like to know more about sleep.
Are we between death and remembering, the fat
track of bedlam, the shiny stairway of hope?
In dreams I love the woman in the golden field,
the woman stooping to wash her feet, the lady
in front of the mirror, the naked back set
against the folds of the sheets. Between the hell
of waking and the tick, tick tock of reality
I hear again the boy bouncing his ball in the
empty garden. Nobody else is there in the garden
of trees and white grass and red flowers. He

is a small lord here in the bending light.
He lets the mystery fall about him. He
gathers hope and trust within his game.

PROPHET OF LOSS

Back in the ordinary days, in real life, he
found words caught him out in speech, in
telling people, in conversation, pages of diary,
paragraphs in novels, stanzas, the hopelessness of
silence. The craft was to let other people say it
all; for him, for themselves. 'Here is the man who
walked on water, split waves, brought truth from
the mountains, came to us across a sea caught in
sunlight. This man dreams our dreams for us. This
man flies. This man is an eagle. He sees the world
from a place beyond our world.' In the cool garden
near to the sea, the old boys talk of cricket and cars
and women with perfect legs.

How God Was Made

I

The first death was eaten.
    The second death was frozen.
        The third death was placed in a cave.
            The fourth death was cast onto water.
                The fifth death was given to flames.
                    The sixth death was hidden in the ground.

When the first death returned
and all life was seen to come again
the oldest men feared what the animals might know.

When the second death was recognised
the oldest men were sent out into winters
longing for ice.

When the third death came back
young children placed flowers near the caves
and learnt to fear the interior darkness.

When the fourth death returned
they waited for people to come out of the oceans
riding on huge creatures, like turtles.

When the fifth death came back and the sixth
these people saw that
flames and the soil
were the same.

The seventh death was put in the sky
where men could not go.
They called it God.

II

They called it God and gave it wings
and gave it their silences and dances.

They called it God and lay down very flat, very small
to reassure it, to show that they would never ignore it.

They called it God and waited for the first interventions
and these they called miracles.

The first miracle was day and light.
    The second miracle was power and pain.
        The third miracle was war and dreams.
            The fourth miracle was other languages.
            The fifth miracles was called night.
                The sixth miracle was the mind of the prophets.

III

Perhaps the prophets were ghosts?
Why did the prophets remind them of birds?
Why did the prophets cling to high places?

And the seventh miracle was madness.

The people who did not respect the God went mad.
The people with ice in their minds, with night in their minds,
with skin like dead crabs, with rubbed-together hands
and ideas shaped wrong and no sense of silence
rocked like birds that were too sick to fly.

The seventh miracle was a curse, a room in rock,
an egg hatching fire, a jabber of bums, snakes
between the virgin's legs.

God held up his mirror and gave them miracles
to keep them noisy
and then went back to his library to invent.

He invented time to make them appreciate
day departing to let in night. He invented words to
make them appreciate power and pain. He invented
smiles so that they could tell the difference between
war and dreams. He invented grammar so that
language could create territories. He created
prophets so that mirrors could be seen in
shallow waters.

And Does the God Pray As Well?

And does the god pray as well, imperfect also,
needing to subjugate the beast, the eternal fear,
the forest on fire in its dreams?

Does the god need light and signs to survive,
a pole to spin hope upon, a hint of magic
when the planets have cooled?

Does the god sometimes pull together its entire might
and count the millions of mistakes and
wonder what the hell is going on?

Time to do the Jesus bit again?
Time for another flood?
Time to close down?

And is it then that this god needs us,
believes in mortals, sends messengers and receives reports,
hungry not for power or recognition or faith

but the small joy of sin?

Coming out of Words

I

Look, I am coming out of words.
These letters are ruins. What we mean
and have said and have struggled
into meaning. 'Many thanks for your meaning.'
'I said that when I wrote again I would be again'
'I now reply to your meaning of July 9th.'
'Your love and kisses were noted and silence
came in between.'
'I have struggled to understand the manner of
your reply.'
Look, I am coming out of words and will
no longer lean on ruins. I dedicate this message
to the sea and pale white bones.

II

No, you cannot change it. Revision means
nothing. Clutter of absurd rituals. The neat
address, the tidy date, the formal declarations,
the clock dripping, the schedule of lines and

lines. Filling the page so that it is at least
a page. Filling a page to conceal a silence.
Filling a page to pull in a reply. Language
on a long haul aginst the yammering of
doubt, the boxes of confusion, the chests of
untidy years.

III

In this cell I see myself as the speaker
into distances, the singer of silences, the
time-teller creating the time that cannot
be told. I counted seasons, I invented beasts,
I retold tales, merged histories and mythologies
so that the alphabet of hours rang against
sleep that was ice or silence or death, dear death.
One man sewed a waistcoat with scraps and
wore a garden. One man invented seven rooms
within one cell. One man changed characters.
One man ate his tongue. One man walked out
and back to America explaining to his ghost
every mile of the way. One man became
his own ghost and lived on after the body
was removed. One man ran at the wall
until he bled to death. But I was a hero,
a speaker into distances, Moses on the run,
a prophet of loss and yonder light, a
priest of fabulous games and images,
a creator of time that cannot be told.
I became Lord Zero, Lord None, Lord
Ice.

IV

Oh look at me not coming out of words,
conforming to these dates and gazes and gesticulations,
the tease of the text, the poise of the poem,
the loud mouth of the popular lie. Do I not
define distances, declare codes, detail density?
This little life now lies down as an epitaph, this little

life now ghosts as a joke, this little death is recalled
in legislation, this little horror now resides in a rule.
Cloak the hope in a neat little joke.
Remember the silence sits up to the sound.
'Tis a gift to be simple' and I am
coming out of words.

V

You did not understand the words
but how did they take to you?
I wonder but do you wonder?
I believe you did not. You did not
do anything. You did not.

You did not understand the words
and in between the page the time
took over, you ran, you hurried,
you made the usual busy motions
and smiled, and smiled.

You knew what you wanted from the poem
on the page, on the eye, on the airs, on
the understanding that image and text
and association and etiquette all fall down
to certain regulations.

Let us give two cheers for such order
but reserve half a cheer for chance
and something for ambiguity and
something over a quarter for
the poison of your arrogance.

VI

Is there life or death in the word
this morning? Can I sleep with the images
of crushed roses? The apples float out on the sea
and on this side of the television screen I see the
apples and the sea and the screen with the small

ornate American lampshade reflected. The apples
move into the lampshade, into the room. The
lampshade enters the sea. This is all done in
seconds of silence, in seas of image and time.
This is the Ten O'Clock News and the announcer
is using wounds again.

Day Comes Again

At Zennor, early light lifting across liquid stone,
lost territory, pathways that disappear
the leaning trees hurrying nowhere.
This church with its own meanings
standing out for a stubborn god, a will that
resists the nonsense of history, the leap of fame,
and a farmer, crunching out into the loud mud
of his yard, shoulders heaving him into the shed,
the day stinking of sacks and pigs and cows,
four bins and unfinished business, worries springing
like coiled wire between the determination, the
roar of storms and the silence of seed. And in this
light, this tide of new day and sea wind,
the hope fastened like a bruise to his soul,
the words against the wounds,
the fingers gripping for miracles, mythologies,
resurrection tricks.

The Sun Belonging to Winter
Poems for American Friends (Spring 1988)

I CORNWALL

Between silence and recognition
the winter entering fields again
and a memory of oceans as if
we flew above them as children.
The stone crops of houses, the walls
in Cornwall falling into old sea,
and always some birds caught out
like rags in a storm of winds.
The sun belonging to that water
rather than to the land. And the
bell of Paul church half here,
half history, a sounding myth
between deep green and the shock
of gorse. Always a surprise. Always
coming back. Pathways that we
believed had disappeared returning
in the spring. The wind as a tide.
The smallest churches with their
forgotten saints. New psalms
from the stutter of our souls.

II ANCIENT CHURCHES

Through ancient glass the light young again,
the mosaic of God's mind soft as grass,
the hands of hope gripping on stone,
the wood of pews polished by prayers.
And the doubt, the scream of ancients,
the gobs stuffed with deceits, the freak
miracles struck in bleeding alphabets,
also here, always present, never past.
At what saint's feet do claws become
straw, the old doubt stars, the ache
of parables angels? Between what we
have and what we hope shall we dance

distortions, shall we sing sweet lies,
shall we make the magic mean? Through
ancient light the truth is always ready
to begin again. Whispers are laws. Our
sound seems sacred. The long procession
of desires makes bells of winds. The sea
is in the sky. The sky is in the silence.
Christ the tiger roams in his poem.

III   BEFORE EASTER SUNDAY

We have lived beyond our faiths.
Coming out of winter we see the sun on
holy stones, ancient light remembers us.
We have become what the stars told us.
Rolling the stone away is essential business;
whatever deceits are revealed, whatever blindness
persists. Water is a miracle in the minds of the
blind. The wind is mosaics. The young
receive our beliefs as ornate codes. What
would we do without these days, this music,
these parables that hang in the mind like truces?
We dig up the meaning, kiss mysteries, place
flowers round the past. The ornate will persists
in its robes, its little dances, its hugs of hope,
its refusals. The days are new dances. We travel
like determined dreamers with secret gifts.
Here is a flower for Lazarus. Here is a token for
Judas. Here is a photograph for angels. Watch out
for the moon behind the trees. The bells are ready again,
to proclaim; to crucify the doubt, the blame.

IV

He has come here to make the god real again.
Between doubt and mosaics of despair he has
to thrust his trust into flames, the white light
of truth, risking absurdity and betrayal. This has
to be done alone. This cannot be shared with others.
The stained glass is not mirrors. The stone silence

constantly falls back and back into comfortable fables.
It is only the mind that leaps forward with its terrible
messages of blood and lies and certainty. The fields
of flowers fall beneath snow. The music is myths.
The stench of prayers bubbles, a trick of light, a joke
of bone, a game deserted by children and saints.
God's wind cannot get in here. There are no birds
here. God's laughter is cut down, defined,
silent as owl flight.

V

God's light. Not the memory of it
but actual, now. This wine of belief.
Grandfather lying in bed, not to sleep
but greeting each day with an hour's prayer.
Each breath in and out a celebration. And
each day in old age taken as God's gift.
Years later finding my mother in the
conservatory talking to the lilies, speaking
to them as healing creatures, faith's flags,
belief's banners, the silence of light
in their furling out, out, into Easter.
Her words as rain. Her passion as sun.
To speak into this flowering as part of it.
And my own silence, the awkward seed,
the winter of my mind, the slow growth,
a green uncertainty that could not sing.
Not to talk of it. Not to take from it.
The years it would take; the digging back,
the certainty of denials and death.
The brilliant heat of the silent lie.

A Message Book

A field message book, 'for the use
of dismounted regiment officers
and non-commissioned officers
of cavalry and infantry',
ruled in quarter-inch squares,
belonging to my grandfather.

> He woke up at five each day,
> cleaned the fireplaces, laid breakfast,
> returned to bed to read the Bible
> from six to seven, heated the
> water for grandmother to wash,
> perused The Times.

'The waterproof cover issued for the
purpose of protecting this book
may be obtained on application.
It should be made to outlast
as many refills as possible.
Special envelopes for despatching
messages, Army Form C.398,
may also be obtained.'

> His study swung between words
> and silence. Some of the silences
> had their own words. Some of
> the words were other forms
> of silences.

'Messages intended for the headquarters of units
and formations will be addressed by the title
of the unit or formation in abbreviated form,
e.g.,   First Army,
             First Div.,
             Seventh Inf. Bde.,
             Second F.A. Bde.'

When he was away at the front
grandfather sent grandmother the
maximum number of letters allowed
written in small handwriting. There
was no waste of space and at the
end of each letter he suggested
chapters and verses from the Bible
that they should both read on a
certain day, at a stated time.

'The abbreviation for general headquarters
will be G.H.Q. The title of the unit will be followed,
if necessary, by the place to which the message
is to be sent. Abbreviations will only be used
when there can be no doubt as to their meaning.
The sender is responsible that any abbreviations
he may use are such as will be understood
by the recipient.'

Sometimes my mother, as a little girl,
would find her mother seated in the garden
with a Bible and a letter in her hand
waiting for the church clock to strike
half past the hour. Then she would
read the passages until it was
time for tea.

'When the message is complete
it will be signed in the right-hand bottom corner,
the rank of the sender, his appointment and the force
he is with being stated. If the message is despatched
by signal this signature is not transmitted, but
is the authority for despatch.'

On leave, grandfather would tell her
something about the living conditions of
the soldiers, about the weather,
about the role of the army chaplain
at the Front. These words, in fact,

said nothing. They were another
form of silence.

'Messages must be as concise as possible,
consistent with clearness, and precise
as regards time and place. Anything
of an indefinite or conditional nature,
such as "dawn", "dusk", "if possible",
"may", is to be avoided. The language
used should be simple...'

When it was over there were
letters to be written, relatives to be
visited, records to be brought up
to date. Each year Remembrance
Sunday appeared like a sad flower.
Flags hung in our church. Grandfather
grew into time. His sermons grew
shorter. He never spoke of the war
at all. Those years became old
letters, dead messages, buried words.
Every so often historians sorted out
the silences from the lies.

Strangers Make Worlds for Us.
Stop. Let the Language Go.

On the other side of sleep
my mother gently. Smiles will not wake
or make it real again. All anger gone.
All sun. All trees. Let the language go.

To remember her smiles, her handwriting
leaping across expensive pages. Smell of
Sundays and the dinner gong ending
Zulu wars and buffalo hunts. Let go.

When our laughter was greatest
sometimes it was her peace. She did
not know how to dance. She often
knew about birds. Away with it.

Beneath that tree in Cornwall
my father's ashes wait. Tall winds.
When she is ready to die we will
be there. There. Because. Become.

Strangers make worlds for us and
hymns and pick up the words into prayers.
We must learn again to do this
and place our faiths in fire.

Look at Her Now

Look at her now, my darling mother,
as she slowly moves away. Her mind
is going out. Her smiles are small songs
that she manages to snatch, to store,
to make a little sense between us.
Inside her body the light increases,
swells past the logic of days.
She is already dancing somewhere else.
We visit her. We are children again.
We long for the toys.

When Did You Last See Your Father?

When it snows, hurrying down the long vicarage drive,
late for a funeral, still with a fag in your mouth;

when it blows, seated reading a detective novel for the
third time in the same damp armchair, the Cornish
wind knocking at the door;

when it freezes, humming a hymn as you feed
the Chinese geese in the apple orchard, the rat
still squatting in the wooden barrel;

when it rains, in words clinging to stones,
incised texts, lichen faiths, flowers
that would become other things;

and when the sun is out
a deck chair
gently askew.

Retreats and Recoveries

I   RETREATS AND RECOVERIES

Not safely within our dreams. Not
facing the faces back, playing at texts and
other games, the furies that we force and fuse.

No longer accepting childhoods, what we
were meant to mean, those briberies of love,
testing the gentle deceits of devotion.

Perhaps discovering the first adult lie, or
more simply a layer of dust cloaking the soul, or
that long box encasing a life in death.

Where did you get to Grandpa? Was God
as good as you created Him or was it all eternal
silences, the everlasting revelation of a mistake?

You were so harsh, so formal to yourself;
perhaps you scared the god away, perhaps
the god didn't need you.

Those early blemishes; the sly wink of
the varicose, the odours of defection, parents
shouting at each other late at night.

And whenever we gathered the images were taken,
the records made, diaries and letters and the visitor's
book binding us into the trite family history.

Running from our fathers so fast that conversation
is painful, the objects awkward, even finally the
words breaking down, smiles stifling.

Our mothers always there with interruptions, intervals,
offering quiet recoveries and truces, the love stretched
between trust and bone and dreams.

Always there, never at the centre, hovering about
my father's obsessions, keeping him amused, white-lying
to herself, determined to self-deceive.

When he went off with young men, ignored her,
totally changed from the reasonable priest, his tirades
no longer disguising the ravages of his need.

Let go; let all this go, so that the
exchange of love and respect can be normal,
the best infecting the memory.

Remembering the light in rooms, the houses
that later turned to ruins, the driveways
crowded with ghosts and dead birds and frogs.

The words entering those rooms, now, to
encounter what is continuing, the living and the
dead holding a conversation, still becoming.

II DAYS AT THE PSYCHIATRIC HOSPITAL

The mornings are ordered, protecting us all
from the anarchies of blood. 'Here will be an old
abusing of God's patience and the king's language.'

Huddled in conformity, out of luck with words, the
patients dribbling in front of television screens;
'poetry is the breath and finer spirit of all language'.

Bandaged against pain, disorder, the threats of memory,
silent visiting hours, attempts to re-enter love;
'In other countries, when I heard the language of my own...'

Each bed an island, each mind a hopeless bird or fish,
each day the repeat of waves and storms; 'If I had loosed
a shaft of language that has flown...'

Here is the buggered history of our universe, the torn
tide, the bleeding jargon, God's broken promises piled
in wounds, 'that such trivial people should muse and thunder...'

And with what words do we come now, to attend
in white, mourning for them, hiding defeat and deformity
behind noise, drugs, gadgets, occasional priests?

Without injury, without discretion, without hope,
what is this hope I offer, do not, cannot;
what are these words doing with us using them?

We are the suppliers of farewells, unspoken goodbyes,
taking them into the gardens, the chapel,
dressing up to sunbathe beneath the cedars.

Let us pretend that we are all humans. Mr Bing
has a right to construct his bridge across the world.
Archie feeds the potted plants sweet, warm tea.

We are the magicians keeping them alive, in doubt
and ruptured, cheating and brilliant pain. Tap, tap of
the memory bone; the fizzle of the spiritual spring.

And if we are doing this at all let us do it well,
learn to love Mr Bing, forgive him over and over,
sing in the chapel this ludicrous truth.

So we lie beneath the cedars, play Bach, let
sun enter deep, never disturb the dreams and
the destinies and the banging doubts.

Mr Bing will die. Tie a label on his toe
and drive with him from the Garden Villa to be peeled back
on the slab. Perhaps a soul will scream.

Mr Bing will be missed. Mr Stone will remember him.
Thirty years on I will still see them staring out
in the snowstorm that enchanted them one April.

III WORDS AS SPACES

Teaching with words, the slow howling hurting
barriers of words, the howling down of words,
the separation of words being defined.

Even stories, slang, pop song, advertisements
become changed, too charged, too cautious
within classrooms, barricades of desks.

Finally I learnt to throw the texts away,
to listen, to get them to tell, to shape it,
to see that it was contact with each other.

In some of the classes we didn't write for weeks;
acting out our own actions and then climbing
into other worlds, creeping out of our own retreats.

Then there was space for understanding. We
needed each other. The alphabet of trust and
recognition was revealed.

'Letters to Giants'. 'Trapped with a Time Bomb'.
'The Floating Man'. 'Killing Parents is Wrong'.
Words as wars, wounds, badges, on the run.

And the poems, at last the poems. Their own
wired images, flashes of soul and bone,
even quietness, even peace.

'The motorbike rose on the hill like
a worry ... his face like a fist ... as
thin as a flea with Asian flu ...'

'My father clings to his seat of silence,
his laughter when he gets drunk
is like jelly made of flesh...'

The words growing in this field of tolerance,
speaking onto the page to make it right, to
catch what you really mean.

The words sometimes so precise they tick
tock, smell, get up and tumble,
suddenly face you with yourself.

The words not as tokens, not texts, not
literary, slowly emerging as being,
as being real, as being ourselves.

And then the gradual negotiation of
spoken word and written revelation and
the ordering of truths.

Desperately attempting to prevent the 'correct',
the neat game of pleasing the teachers,
the damage of the red adult pen.

IV WHAT ARE THE POETS FOR?

The life and language engaging extremes;
pulpit persuasions, words as holy birds, and
Tennyson's charge crackling from the past,

so that mistakenly place and age make meaning memorable
until one is so startled by the reality of this activity,
words as wounds and bared confessions.

Then the land and purpose change, what we are
doing here with these words changes us, the
ordering and re-ordering of our searching.

What are the poets for in this motion and
emotion to express, celebrating and confusing
architectures of the soul?

What we see is not what we feel, is not
what we say we are saying, finding a voice in
palaces and prisons of the intellect.

At the end of each idea there is a silence
waiting to chew back along the dotted line
to begin again,

or between howls and hallelujahs we hear
tap tap the sticks of doubt
stopping everything that we valued.

Biting off more than we knew, hurting
ourselves and our friends; unsure about success,
dreading rebuke and blocks.

Sometimes attempting between flight and originality
the brutish new direction of slang, obscenity,
a blunt Catullus thrust.

But then Crane leaps, Berryman jumps,
Thomas bombards his brain with booze, the famous
die and cheat themselves.

Gently we roll the diction, split prosody and
warn ourselves of greatness. To discover truth
between an error and a dream.

Whose language have we become when
the singing gets outside our head,
jostles others, never protects?

What do we think we could do to
ourselves, between the orchards of childhood
and the waiting rooms with views?

In the winter park I can see myself
reading a poem, writing something down, catching
light between unseen stars.

A Separation
for Clare and Emily

Between trees and bells and what we have called lives
a separation of this day and that; a loss, a gain.
Whose ideas are these anyway, the desk and close shapes
or the running, amazed, lilting tricksters?
What may have appeared to roar now merely rattles
and we are left with old letters, pencil ends, the images
of litter when we longed for the folding patterns of flowers.
And this is not to be misunderstood; it is not a failure;
we attempt these songs to make an opera; hear us still.
Or we begin to re-arrange such observances, to bring
into their formations, to see a new alphabet of desires.
Beneath ancient trees the earth assembles, collects, gives
out from the promise, surpasses what might have betrayed.
Between familial ghosts we seek renewals, assurances and

just so much mystery between the carols and the challenges.
You can do anything you want between the power to create and
the prophecy, the parades and retreats of faith, the certainty
of doubt. Light upon life so that belief is another way
of seeing yourself before you can even begin to speak.
Gathering in these things from what began as secrets;
the runner in the mist appearing to disappear; losing it
and gathering it; the sound of children in imagined gardens.
Again I see my grandfather in his early morning room,
reading from Genesis again, the entire reading ahead
of him, the five a.m. room, the holy room, the
light surrounding this hour of grace, its hymn.
What did he do to settle his life, to survive
such certainty, the problem of pain, spending so much
between these orderings of words and the promised kingdom?
Was it love, finally driven by agony, welcoming its hold?
Inside this life all such memories of other lives and ways, these
entrances and entreaties; a chair on the lawn to bring back
the dead, a clock that still sounds, the rumour of ritual;
my wife with Quaker hands and a Cherokee forehead;
my eldest daughter with her American grandad's German nose.
Voices behind the voices that we hear. Mirrors fading into
the rhyme of time. One looks out from the railway carriage
window and sees where the trees must have been. They were there
when we were not. Their existence itself has been transformed.
In a certain place there is no longer certainty, there is no time
for time. Logic is lunatic and the Fairy Feller falls
on his dreams. Silence. Did you hear it? Silence.
Is this the music of it or memory from the grass harp?
Over and over into coils of recognition; loss begun;
the speech we use with eyes or hands or other tapestries.
My father in his final garden wanting the roses to grow so tall
they could only fail. Frail flags for his dreams. Impossible
flames of his obsessions. In winter even he was still
bringing rotting balls of petals into the house, and those lilting
tokens to place between the Christmas decorations.
And years before my mother had nourished the lilies,
frail nuns not used to dancing, holy flame throwers,
the furl of light breaking, a wave, a wave.

She stood in the Somerset conservatory to watch
their huge awakening and in summer they were transplanted
to the walled-in garden. It was two days of labour.
In holy week they were so carefully cut, laid in baskets
and taken to different churches to become Easter lights, the
shade of hallelujahs, the shape of praise, the blooms
of resurrection miracles, God's brilliant bunting.
A wave, a miracle, the silent roar of their applause.
God's dancers between what we would say and how we
might dream; doubts making beautiful retreats between
promises and stone signs and psalms of ancient light.
It was there. It is still there. It is always possible. My
mother's hands put down the roots again in late September.
What will become of the glory of lilies placed in the damp
dark to await winter, their new time, their new light.
In other people's lives, forward and back again,
the rock of uncertainty, the agreement to take what we
believe we understand and communicate. The belief in words,
the chorus of texts, the fiction with one's truths.
Token within the song within the certainty within the fears
of disbelief. Reading the texts so that we too can begin,
translating faith and making it future. Where are we
in this time and is it simply tribute, a cradle of
cheers and cautions? Discovering the tiny spider's nest
or the newborn mice under the slab before the dog
comes, the thunder returns, the anxious reality bangs
down its fist. Where do we hide in seeking revelations?
After my father's sermons how do I approach the questions,
grown past his certainty and my emotions? Each question
is seen as revolt, a compulsion, a hurtful mosaic.
He has become his text, refuses to talk, cannot
retrace the journey, sees no respect in this activity;
the words are barriers, walls, appalling flags.
I see my father in the autumn garden. It can
never be spring with him. Fifty years later he is
still recovering from his mother's death. Family diaries
do not simply record. In the attic in an ornate trunk
her dresses and letters waiting. The images waiting. The smell

waiting. Hung up in time the love pressed into his life
like a huge blossom. Her world within his world but
the words failing, the memory distorting now, the image
not yet released. Token within the song gone wrong.
Our own music constantly moving from the formal purple
of geranium to the compelxity of green. When the flower
is done we see the leaf again, the new surrounding plants.
And it is always light; here the winter light
falling like time's ghosts to ripple history; here the
morning of gardens in spring, the uncoiling hosts
of white blossom; driving across from Zennor
the rat, the rat, the rat with its hat, the
rat in the rain with its Zennor hat, the rat,
the rat with its Zennor hat and that is that.
Late at night the August garden heavy with
moon, with the conversations locked away,
the walks between trees, the deck chairs stacked
as if we folded each day to bring it out again,
to erect our dreams of summer days, the
mower in the shed, clinging to its sweat
and oil, the gardener's hands grabbing birds
caught in the fruit cage netting to let
them fly or tightening, tightening on the
moss soft throats. Small deaths. Small
passings. The last of light in those clasps.
The Zennor bell is wind and rain. The Paul bell
is light across these fields of stone and wild.
The sea is bells, heavy with loss and chaos,
heaving retreats and rituals, storms of chance
and courage, weed tides where we have not been
curling so deep. Into our dreams of seas, our stories
rolling to legends; saint's bones and lonely beliefs,
as if all myths collected here, the chime of chains.
On bright cliffs crowds gather to watch the sun
fall from the sky, before we leave this
to memory and snapshots. Before the Zennor rat
discovers its trap and makes its decision. Before
the small alarm clocks come out to command again;
a few shells and sea smoothed glass are hidden

in the tuck box or a pencil case; a perfect
pebble is carried into winter as if we could
never trust and returning be the exact same.
At St. Just in Roseland we visit my father's
grave after six years and walk down to
the water as if his message were waiting.
What have we done to the time, the
meanings, the inheritance? What values
have ceased? How can this small stone
contain our dedications? We come here
to make a record of ourselves, our lives,
as if he recognised such distance,
and sensed such separations. Does it matter
at all; is it trust or loss to be here now?
Seated at his desk I do not look into his eyes.
His last letter is filed in time, the crazy typing
still smudged, the misunderstanding still in print,
the distortions a territory never to be settled now.
What was loss is still loss, there is no way now.
Seated in his swivel chair with the small brass
inscription I can still hear his commands as we
packed the car, looked back at the sea, saw
him looking back at us, an entire month
photographed in the rear mirror review. Let
your light so shine (the bell to toll);
let your light (the bell across the fields
and the sea and the stone of fallen villages);
let your light so (the ocean's bells never
heard above the green parade of tides);
let your lives, your words, your silences
so become this peace, this love, this
separation in order to remember what was
real, what was attempted, what was imperfect
but sought; let this peace so love;
let this speech so save us; let these
bells of recognition survive our dreams;
looking into the eye, the time, the desperate
will to become not certain but believed.

Two Weeks after My Father's Death We Pick the Pears

Two weeks after my father's death we pick the pears from five trees.
My mother wanted to leave them but here I am swinging in this tree.
The pears are ready. We have timed it just right.
Old bark bruises my back; green dust gets into my sweat.
I work until the moon starts its first rattle across the sea.

Each pear is handed down and inspected by my mother.
Kneeling on the steps she places each fruit in a box.
Every pear has to be looked at carefully. There is order
here and some craft.

There is no time to be afraid. In the coming months
I can see her treating letters, papers, words, memory
in the same way.

Enter the Hundred Women

Some wore tall hats for the sadness of their lives,
others roses to remind them of secrets
and a few, who never spoke, wrapped
the shapes of early evenings
across their shoulders.

And there were whores, expensive women, rich
ladies who could only parade;
each jewel bore a man's name, each smile
recorded the death of a dream; small
dogs scuttled between their legs.

The old ones, used to symbols, raised
their faces as if ghosts observed, cared, could
still be of use; their handbags were stuffed
with letters and playing cards and
photographs of the dead.

And the last to enter, to roll forward as
a wave, were the cripples, the deformed, those
with faces like paper bags. They were wonderful.
They came to the front of the stage to bow,
to whisper what they knew about Lorca.

from *Turtle Mythologies*

It is Raining Between the Words

It is raining between the words
so she does not see them
between flowers and the switched off world
and meals that she never forgets to enjoy
and the priest once told me how at communion
she remembered every word of the Lord's Prayer
but she failed to remember me
or had put me somewhere else
perhaps with the new shoes in the box
or between the folds of biscuit wrapping
or was it for me she set out the tea things
waiting for us to come
knowing so well that each day
the world was getting a little
younger?

What We Came to Say

It begins with earth, within excavation and
redistribution, an exchange of geologies, the
old outlines hunted now by light, fraction by
fraction the new identities dug out by mind.

Within exact dimensions, a trigger of tokens,
the new vibrating against necessary traditions,
and the essential fictions of truth, a new way
of assessing where sun discovers the darkness of gold.

And the people, coming here with confidence and codes,
their need to build above the doubt, the comfortable,
something beyond wonder and loss, technologies confronted
with riddles that can collapse in a prayer.

Finally a ceremony that defines what was meant,
what we came to say, the radiant struggle
cast into glass, wood, stone; God's light tall
as a miracle, quiet as bird bone.

What we came to say as founded in
the very first few words of the priest, the initials
of faith in the first amen, begun in the
hoop of the prayer as the circle of hope rose;

each one of us creating our own god, our own
acceptances, telling ourselves certainties so that
the wind howl and demon doubt and sting of sin
fall down, blur, scatter in the sense of love;

God's reality spun between brass and glass, each
image unique in its meanings, the bells that
called us here telling those who would not attend
that after the silence there are ways of replying;

a very gentle communion.

Words to Disturb the Silence

The Poet and the Priest have both listened with the silence
very long times. One is working from the silence into words and
the other from the words that should shock us into silence.
Somewhere in between lies truth's rage, its ragged fiction, its
itch to get us going out across the frozen terrain or
lighting a fire in the centre of the forest. Somewhere alone
the Priest surrounded by other people's furies. Somewhere else
the Poet in the room rattling with beasts and mythologies.
Somewhere the words hidden by ice or fire and the great
pressure of intellect to force out the demon or diamond.
So the Poet prepares his mind to face the page of white
as it fills with attractive images and firm enough sounding lines.
So the Priest fighting to design his own identity in a swirl
of liturgy and other people's syntax and the massive impression
of God's scrawl. And the Poet sees it is possible to grip
from the disturbance small undertakings and trusts. And the Priest
sees grass and earth and blood falling from the effigies of Christ.
And at moments when they have sensed the passage of
new planets they are given words to disturb the silence for
seconds only. Then must begin again, begin to listen again.

Another Summer

When we have left the lawns and conversations
some of us enter the orchards, already smelling of autumn.
But it is still summer, tall dreams and the accordion
player at country fairs and in Ireland my cousin
dancing in a field of deep, green moon. They have
always written to us saying this is the real life. And
I recall on Sundays the dogs also coming to church.
But now it is another summer. We stroll into these
English orchards and remember the seas of August. The
trees are sometimes so low they carry the aroma
of storms in their bark, the silence of ancient stars.

Mythologies of the Heart

I

Entering the green bedroom, early morning, Sunday,
on all fours, the grandfather clock in the hall suddenly ticking
so loudly, about to strike five;

odour of stale bread, shoe leather, the huge bed like a ship of
comfort, but not being sure, the welcome concealed somewhere in sheets
blankets, eiderdown, the stern drawl of my father's snore;

the small escapade now crumbling into a ball of uncertainty, the game
slipping as I crawl beneath the bed, sense the dusty springs above me,
my legs brushing against slippers, a copy of *The Times*;

deciding to stay put, concelaed in this terrain, until the cold will
force me out, covered in dust and small feathers, back to my room;
the tent so still, the company of dead men, the creaking ice.

II

One   – is the view of my parents' car as it departs along the school drive
              leaving me standing beside the tuck box, other pupils dashing past.
Two   – is the prefect called 'Dickie' telling me to get a move on,
              the chaos of conformity as I line up for the first roll call.
Three – is the hush in the dining hall as the house master enters,
              the eyes of the senior girls searching for tears.
Four   – is the loudness of the chaplain as he howls out the school
              hymn, his certainty like a slap of paint across the face.
Five   – is the dormitory and name tapes on everything, the matron stiff
              as a toothbrush, the methodical inspection of testicles.
Six   – is the silence of lights out, sliding deep into the igloo
              of one's bed, dreading already the six-thirty bell.
Seven – is the guessing of names, the will to belong, the instinct
              to survive, the dash to get it right and over with.
Eight – is the first letter from home, the odour of mother's writing paper,
              the image of the dog missing me already.
Nine   – is the first cross-country run, amazed to be placed in
              the first dozen, a small chirp of pride.

Ten   – is a roar of laughter as Dunn puts on his jock strap
        the wrong way round.

        And I still feel the water in the rock pool in Cornwall
        I attempt forty lengths, the tiger stripes of the sun;
        I turn and plunge, the entire summer puckering in prisms,
        my mother waiting with the towels and coffee, smell of
        doughnuts and the salty dog.

Easter Poem for My Daughters
For Clare and Emily; Good Friday, 1990

At Salisbury, in April, the figure of a woman
energetically striding out towards the town, the
cathedral behind her, tourists on either side
and workmen erecting three crosses on a platform.
She hurries to help, to participate, to belong. There
is no time to doubt, to linger on interpretations.
And across Wiltshire we have seen the white horses
and walked between the stones at Avebury;
it is said that the devil will speak to anyone who has
run one hundred times round his chair. The light
of ancient custom still hunches between these
sentinels. And today, Good Friday, the long day,
a hundred people processed in witness in cold rain
before we sang the hymns and reached out for truths.
Truths? What are we doing with these ideas and fables
and what should I say to you when you accompany
us out of respect, simple guilt? We have all
done this, following our parents's faiths, not
believing any more but anxious to touch the
base of something that once made us happy.
Afraid of burying the God. Afraid of not even
doing that. Fearful of setting aside not
only the cermonies but the energy of essential doubts.

The Sadness of Policemen

The sadness of policemen is always there;
just when you were about to get the deckchairs out
a soft blow of snow. And there behind the priest's
dull cassock we glimpse his terrible, boyish green socks.

To enter this room and look towards our dreams of seas;
far off a ship is sinking, a jolly fellow stuffs a puffin
in a bottle. The trick is to burn the strings and seal
the torso in before the gong for breakfast sounds.

And the sadness of policemen hangs about the house
like a bad meal, a spoilt joke. Listen; you can hear
the poor people of Africa hunting for lice. The old
lady has a bell in her bag. When it dies she will ring.

Between the winter trees hundreds of men freeze in the rain.
Their hair longs for cottage fires, their hands guzzle like fish.
They watch a space in a field, they have done this for days.
This is called training for sadness and it is essential.

Sister Murphy Leaves for the New Life

Leaving the farm; ah, that is what I am doing now.
I am doing this thing of dread now, dreamed of years and years.
I go out from the house that is emptied now, into the yard
that I hardly recognise. The place where the dog always waited
is no longer there with the dog. The dog has taken it away.
So it is with the rook tree, the pig house; the byre quite
empty now. It has all flown down to ruin. The fields race
into the sea and my boys cannot any longer come home to here.
There is no place to be here now. So I sit in the van and
crammed between the little man from nowhere and the priest
I go out with them to the lane that becomes a road that
becomes the hills. It does not take so very long. It takes

about two marriages and five boys and the baby that still
cries in my mind in the night. I hold tight to that
child as we leave all that now. These shoes are all wrong.

An Idea of Light at Lake Como

I

Pliny knew this light
boasting of his villas at Bellagio,
one so close to the waves
'almost as if you were in a boat'.

The same density exposing these trees
that appear to rise up from the water
into a structure of beams, rays,
as if everything ascended;

villas, gardens, hotels, parks, even
the boats attempting to blossom on the
lake; an entire geography still ringing
with the ancient granite wound.

Only the guessed at centre of the lake
reflects a finite surface, a held fusion,
not possible to locate exactly, confusing our
view; a shard of ice, a glacial shadow.

The light rises, part of a perpetual code,
a passage. We attempt to catch it on
surfaces, stones, window panes; we even
believe in imitating such energy.

Surfaces are studied, traced across stone,
carved across canvas and wood, refracted;
images of light never surpassing the reality,
isolating us in the meaning of our time.

II

The bell of San Giacomo times our days;
the tourists meeting history on their own terms,
setting out on small journeys, clutching texts and
schedules, facing the faces of stones, doves of culture.

Even our speeches to God are timed, limited;
light rises within each message; passions become
pacts; mosaics help us fly; bells boom back
realities and drinks are served beneath the lime trees.

Each evening we meet on the roof garden
as the water folds time; sunsets beat gold and
the single star slips behind the mountains, our
knowledge, our ability to explain.

III

We have so arranged our days that between
the late breakfast and purchasing the day-old paper,
the visits to villas and churches and gardens, the essential
siesta and avoiding having to speak to other guests,
buying new film for the camera, that it is only in
the time between evening and night we comment again
on the light around the lake, the actual lake.

At nine p.m. in late June
the water has become the light
of the sky. The sky has become
the lake. The land has risen
above the light. The lake
sings stone.

IV

Pliny wrote home about this.
He sent a postcard to a girl in Chicago,
about the evening coming on, the suddenness
of night, the lake entering one of his villas,
his dreams.

Pliny saw a great future here, by the lake
at Bellagio; he purchased several villas and
did them up and dreamed of hotels with small
coffee tables and the trees all the time
climbing into the sky.

V

Oleander now discovers it power
to pierce the night, the lake folding over and over,
petals of certain darkness.

Two stars only in the sky, and in one of the villas
yucca blooms its porch light, the moon
hidden by an ocean of cloud.

Even now, in June, the mountains clasp snow;
behind the mountains, Switzerland, behind
Switzerland the world.

Before sleep, before sleep, we see the arum lily
within its own glow in an overgrown garden;
a wild thing now; a banner of blossom
telling a story nobody wishes to hear.

The villa will soon be a ruin but
her life is there; old lady in the villa
somewhere, in a back room. The comfort

of lime trees, oleander, the single lily,
a fusion of what has been meaningful and
what each day has become.

The oleander perches in its green world,
a thousand white birds ready to fly.

VI

Not in cascades, robes,
but the light in this place centred,
precise on a table with a blue vase
in a courtyard at the rear of San Giovanni;

as if to prepare one for entering,
by a side door, into an absence of light,
the eye and mind at once humbled,
as if an old secret had been proffered;

so that all we comprehend initially
is the gold of the altar, one's senses drawn
up; waves into waves, pooling, gold
into silver into gold;

and now the white flowers below
the altar cloth flow, pool, fuse also;
tides of light as if the outer darkness
could be drained by faith;

drawn off, trawled, so that nothing
but this high ocean exists.

VII

The nun in her white of silence
who walked under the lime trees each afternoon
now strolls across the garden, over the path
and continues across the lake itself;

and now the gardener in his dark blue shirt
follows her, still raking the leaves, the surface
of the lake, its snake skins and petals
of gold;

and the wedding guests follow
the bride and groom across the formal lawns
to walk on water, to enter this idea,
to embrace all things with
flowers in their hands;

and the head waiter at Hotel du Lac
rides his green motorbike onto the lake:
already he can see the dinner tables
set out for the guests;

the peach tablecloths are so distinct,
the wine glasses shine,
the vases of flowers
are arranged perfectly;

and bells.

Returning

Odysseus

Finding the old man in the garden, he stood
a short distance to observe where the years had marked,
time taken, the place itself begun new creation stories.
And, just as he had anticipated so long, acting out and
rehearsing in the tall nights, he was more terrified of the
moment to come than any great challenge or adventure.
The words that might fail, the stories that so easily
misinformed, the abuse of rumour. And so now, knowing
that he could no longer restrain the moment, he stepped
forward to let the old man see him beneath arched trees;
this ancient man who appeared so weak now, so lost, no
longer protected by status and ritual. And as he held
his father in his arms, after the small cry of recognition,
the waiver of the brain lasting seconds only; and as he
held his father beneath those ancient trees as if without

him the torso would fail, would fall, it was as if he
clutched light and wisdom and self-recognition, as
if seas and storms, battles and speeches fell away.
And it was said that when the old man went to bed
that night he could still feel the strength of his son's
arms like huge sea surges, image mingling within
image, and that outside in the garden the trees
spoke his son's name again and again: 'Odysseus, Odysseus;
he has returned'. And all that night the old man's mind
rippled mosaics.

Hallelujah

Is this where the angels come, early by the sea,
on the cliff tops staring down at the green?
Is this where temptation and experience fizzle out,
where silence is the essential dialogue of forgiving?
All the old tunes fade here, all the tattered orthodoxies
topple over, all time's lies lose their fizz.
Ideas rise like kites, imagination breeds eagles,
small bells of recognition call us to belief.
This is where the angels come,
early by the sea, between gulls and stars,
between days and distortions,
between love and healing,
between voices and desertions,
between what we will call miracles and truths.
Now they are dancing.
Now they are setting down their visions.
Now they are getting out their trumpets and their banjos.
Now they are trying on their make up.
Are they perhaps clowns? Or is that they
seek between the solemnity, the sermons,
the sacred numbers and the holy codas,
God's private sign, his recognition, his
laughter; staring at the seasons, the

planets; envying the fast cars,
the motorcycle boys; whistling slow anthems,
humming hallelujahs?

Turtle Mythologies

On a shore we cannot reach
turtles begin their journey to another continent
that is essential to the meaning of our history.
They pass midnight swimmers and pleasure boats
and later fishermen whose lights encircle the dependable green.
They pass corals and outer islands and dolphin playgrounds
the ocean gradually becoming dark stars, tiger moons,
far beneath them an endless mosaic of broken bells.
They pass the drowning man's final dreams and the place
where sharks were killed. They pass the immense wreaths
of wrecks. They pass what had been an island village.
They pass the point of recognition, memory, challenge,
identity; intuition pulling them on, the brilliant legend
of their beings giving them energy. They pass from glimmer
of green and shots of silver into deepest grey and gold. They
hear whale song, the nudge of chains, beatitudes
of oysters, the surge of volcanoes, the shift of dunes.
Sometimes, far above them, there is a storm or an iceberg
grates, or a submarine waits with its barbaric store.
Sometimes they have to detour rags of atomic filth,
packages of poison, containers and barrels leaking
death and texts of hate, rags of rage and ruins of abuse.
Sometimes they have to summon up greater determination
to survive these places, these cruel creeds. In these territories
it would be easy enough to turn back or simple expire, yet
they pass through these passages, they travel on and forget,
they uphold their culture and keep stretching into the
brightness that is waiting beyond them. They are entirely
compelled by the future, the promise of new continents,
the tides of new becoming, carols of bright beaches

and surging stars, the dawn that must wait for them
and their message, their testimony. Sometimes the intuition of
this becomes so great it rides like waves of stars,
and they hear the dolphins urging them on and the green rolls
into gold. Sometimes they hear their ancestors calling them
to become, to create a new world, to enter the meaning
of our history, the planets ordering them to rise and surface.
They pass beyond oceans and lands, surfaces and forms, the
fundamental and the ecstatic, the mission and the meaning,
beyond what had been their purpose, beyond their history,
beyond time and recollection and structure, beyond fusion and
miracle, beyond symbol and data, beyond the God and His
vision, beyond star time and planet pulse, beyond angels
into a map of mythologies.

from *Dancing With Bruno*

Now that My Mother No Longer Comes to Me

Now that my mother no longer comes to me,
her words, advice, the quiet wisdom, always ready to
forgive and apologise and move on to the more important thing;
I have to make her from silences, fragrances, and it
is easy enough. In Albania, in an old people's home,
I sat in the lonely, rocking room with ancient grandmothers
who hung between dreams of children and mountain villages.
And I made my mother there. And later, in Croatia,
I heard the church bell and saw the old women
leaving dark buildings to walk to a place of light.
And here, in England, where the ritual has all
but broken the passion, I see old women who are
still strong, still passionate, holding on to desire.
Now that my mother no longer comes to see me I have to
greet these women as though they were my mother's sisters,
knowing that in me they remember their sons, their husbands,
even their fathers who were silent about love but in

a late spring garden or in a farm field fused by the
need for visions, the certainty in their stride a
communication past texts and prayers and entrances.

Memories of the Duke

The Duke is a sad man and always wears rain.
He is waiting for the telephone to be installed,
but first of all it has to be invented.
He says we must plant more trees or
we will shortly run out of birds.
The Duchess, when she was there, sold
his history and took her meals in the garden.
Even in winter. She said bushes made more sense
than babies and only closed the grounds on Christmas Day.
The Duchess, when she was there, said
the Duke was soiled and past pruning;
and what was the point of autumn?
And when the Duchess was not there,
when oh when she had gone, when some mad monk
had spirited her away in a wheelbarrow of stars
and mulch, when the clocks had all stopped and
the Duke was able to descend from his rocking horse,
he could amble from room to room
completing other people's conversations,
recounting anecdotes and the beginnings of jokes,
fumbling for his old identity, urinating
onto the azalea beds and generally
misbehaving from a very great height.
The Duke is a sad man and always wears rain.
He is waiting for the telephone to be installed,
but first of all it must be invented.
He says we must plant more birds or
we will shortly run out of trees.

Still Life

We live longer than our parents,
moving on, no longer able to linger at certain places,
the small moat filled in, the tennis courts built on,
content to carry these images that are no longer truths.
Festivals may bring them back, hurrying across the years
to marriages and funerals, family feasts and even failures;
or in the children's dressing-up box a waistcoat or top hat
reappears tapping out its trite reconciliations. Unlike
the photographs, the oil paintings, which are too ordered,
even the ones that get stored in the silent roof space
and only come out when we pack to move house. Meanwhile
somebody's painting up the antique cradle and my daughters are
raiding my shirts and somebody wants to borrow a bow tie.
In the hall the umbrellas seem to belong to strangers and
the walking sticks have collapsed from fashion it seems.
In the summerhouse a basket of bowls, like abandoned
prehistoric eggs, lightly covered in web,
reminding one of perfectly flat lawns
and the moment late afternoons curled into evenings.

Autobiographical

To write a poem, that doesn't have oceans
or my father walking all over it. No priests
without prayers, the slow bell of doubt, or
those dark towers beside ancient tides.
Oceans again, conversations that repeat themselves
in the late hours, knock knock on the knowledge
of dreams. Or my father walking all over it.
The old girls of Greece or Ireland
where a dance in a field leads to truth
or other loves. Or Sam Frost still bending
the hedgerows in Bedfordshire, his blood on the
billhook, snow even when the sun shines.

The brilliance of childhood, the light inside
the church before the worship begins. Before
anything begins to be.

Swimming to America

Somebody is always closing a door to a room,
opening a window, preparing a birthing table,
remembering a place in the earth. The rain and sun,
light and darkness have entered and retreated
before and between our worlds and silences. Our seasons
of being are inherited, passed on, done.
Sometimes there is a shade that persuades in
a different manner, or the phrase is perceived in
a changed code; what we had considered as
custom halts us, is original.
The expectation is seldom this. We are
busy with histories, translations of small
events, and our memories are crowded with ancestors.
The voice of a grandfather is present each Christmas
and even when they have moved on the games of
children remain in the secret gardens or ruins of trees.
And the future itself is made this way.
It is grown in the closing of a door to a room,
in the action of opening a window, at the moment
of choosing a name or an inscription. The light
passing beyond us. The noises of this planet already
tossed into galaxies. Each day somebody attempts
this little dance in the jungle and catches up with
an ancient revelation, begins a journey that is
merely another route, puts on the wings of mystery,
dreams of swimming to America, heading out
beyond the moon and the ocean's impulse and the
places where once there were other gods.

Three Types of Silence

I THE SILENCE OF EDWARD HOPPER

It is good to be here, isn't it?
The sun making us real, the snow ageing us;
winter's tale timing us all.
Each lull is real, uninterrupted, us;
being alone we make a crowd. No bar tender
or Mister or white lean legs will change
our histories. Passing by, out, over is our
profession. There's nobody to leap up, go crazy,
get God or greatness here.
Our confessions are creaks. Our blasphemies are
harmless farts. Sometimes the sun sets between
one dream and another and it's only the quality of
despair that keeps us coming here.

II THE SILENCE OF WILLIAM CARLOS WILLIAMS

A dance
                    he said
as assurance –
                    the natural
display and embrace –
                    the simple
utterance of an orchard
                    when we
have left it
                    going home
across these fields
                    talking of
friendships –
                    waving
farewells.

III THE SILENCE OF FARMERS IN WINTER

Out there; not even their dreams visit
out there. Dogs whine near the barn. Rain
keeps the pigs in. This is the time of radio days

and television people and the roar of football crowds.
Not even the dreams go that far down, to visit
the boles and the roots.
Out there the wind is white, the moon a blister.
When a tree comes down it opens up a cavern
that smells of dead water and nettle. The farmers
think of this and words in boxes and of weddings in the
old days, the tables laid out with fruit and flowers
and the women whispering of sunsets.

Seasons of Light

Light folds between apple boughs;
in winter you can sense its crisp decays.
Between storm and snow it gathers deep,
waiting for April and a new song.

In summer it enchants thousands of trees;
in night orchards the bark is still warm.
Core's convulsion shapes each fruit as if
this time could never come again.

In early autumn apple pickers visit with baskets
and ladders. Gently they lay the fruits in the boxes.
In silence the reek of former seasons settles them;
odours of twine, old paint jars, dead nests.

My grandfather told us once that apples were
only ready when they came away with a simple twist.
As a boy I was sent high into the branches seeking
out those we could not reach or shake away.

At Christmas the red ones were polished and placed
in ornate cut-glass bowls. At the table white flesh
yielded to ivory handled knives; deep, deep,
the memory and seasoning of summer days.

from *An Alphabet of Light*

I AND DOES IT REALLY MATTER?

And does it really matter? The trees reflecting, the lake
in shaking quilts. Patterns perfecting all the time. Reality
and then reflection and then what reality we make of that reflection.
A surface view. What we say of it and to it. Talking out
of the normal recognitions, that is the natural self; the way
we say it is the way we see it is the way we believe it.
And does it really matter that this is what we do, today,
and passing on this is memorised to a point of poetic self?
This remains; the trees reflecting on the lake in shaking quilts
and we are also in this scene, to be here and become this scene,
to inhabit what otherwise would be. Those who pass by are now
extras in an evolutionary impulse that we keenly recognise.
So; there are the groups on benches who say the words that
we don't actually hear but allude to. There are
the dark cut outs of rooks as they ring their territory.
A woman and a dog, a cyclist, the passers by who only do
that from our perception. Traffic from a distance. The
formal park and its definitions; lake, loggia, temple
in the woods, closed cafe, symmetry of pathways and
sundial and flower beds. The red setter roaring in
this sun. And the words that are here and that are
surface. All the gesticulations that are flags of the
familiar. The branches of these trees coming out of
water, mass of shade and silhouette and essence
of energy reflecting in the substance of light
and no light and this yield of water. The surface
of the lake. A view of the edge of the lake. A view.
Surfaces and depths and the dimension that we
contribute to this. The sun surrounding the running dog.
In the memory now a view of trees surfacing, cascading.

II BECAUSE YOU ARE NOT USING THE WORDS

Because you are not using the words we do not hear from you.
Yes; you are here and we are here but the distance is becoming the silence.
Within your nowhere words, their shining shambles, their swoons, we are

trying to hear you, we knock on the edge and something rattles, we attempt
to get behind the jabber in this room, this nest that you have built.
You are still our mother as we seek to mother you; fail to reach,
cannot even sing your songs. Initially in front of the television thing you
clapped-on the wrestlers, then applauded the weather man, sang at
The News. Now it is not here. Switching off our world you are in
Ipswich as a daughter, you are in Islington as a health inspector,
you are driving a car to Dover to get to France, you are picking
mountain flowers in Switzerland. Now you are out there all the time
between these and those. Sometimes a page that was flicking past
holds, flies up, is a curious bird of slight recognition.
Tea must be prepared. The parents will need their tea, expect it.
Soon they will come up to kiss you goodnight. We do not exist in
this story. Our names do not exist. There is no bookmark. Pages
hurl through spaces and places and finally create silences again.
Last week you told us that we must get in the car for France.
You packed us in the back and set off into the roar of
roads and I suppose we all arrived. But who were we and what
have we become? When I found you on the floor you said
you had fallen from a horse and must get back for the bells.
Were these the bells of Norwich; church bells or school bells?
In the afternoon light you linger in your tree. In this nest
we have placed some photographs and water colours and now you
are telling me about your child, the one with the problem
spine, and how he, how he, how he. The window opens
onto a coastal view. Soon the festive lights will spill
across the bay. 'I am just going into an in. Pock. Pock.''.

V   EDGE OF MADNESS
For Tom and Alastair

Edge of madness, edge of being.
'Shoot at slow intervals until I order you to stop.
Shoot them until they can't sleep. Don't stop until
they are on the edge of madness.' Ratko's killing
credo. Mladic's madness as well. When the war ends
and the news of war passes into history you had better tell
the people because the noise of war has made them deaf.
You had better tell them because they have filled their

bedrooms with terror. Because at the edge they saw
no way forward and the world behind them was already dead
and they are the dead; Ratko's dead. Between the living
and these dead the distance is a scream, a sniper, a landmine.
Welcome to Sarajevo. Welcome to Hell. Welcome to Ratko's
Alley, as you peer out between derelictions, as you stare
at the sun in somebody else's sky, as one thousand days
burn, as the gravedigger hunts for space in the mud,
as you weep between stone's blood, as Melika
Vareshanovic strides out in her best dress and pearls
between the sandbags and the soldier and the shadows
of Serbs, as the silent playgrounds entertain the wind,
as the girl runs towards her mother's embrace as she
squats on her stumps, as the head of a doll smiles
out from the wreck of a truck, as the library blazes.
The flames reach each book in turn, run fingers
along each shelf, delve into chapters of life
as it was. The words on millions of pages become
fire and the wind lifts the words and they begin to
fly out into the city, into the ruins, into the
madness. For a while even the people's words are
on fire; edge of meaning, edge of being.

VI   FATHERS ARE MOVING THROUGH
MOURNINGS OF LIGHT

Fathers are moving through mournings of light. They have
been here before and know where the wonder begins. They don't
tell you this but give you stories and customs and when it is
a special day they sprinkle riddles on your bed to wake
you up. Wake up the wonder. Wake up the splendour.
Fathers are always doing this between the work and the weeping
and the sad songs and the silences and the hunting for lost
things. They all do this; hunting in the eyes of their wives,
in the prayer once it has been said, in the backs of
Bibles and in the fullness of the wine. You can see them
staring into a field for something we may become. You can
see how they attend to the accounts of heroes as if there
were something to be inherited there. They listen to the

stories of fallen men like Custer and Scott
as if there were some missing trick. They laugh with us as
Charlie Chaplin collapses again and again and yet behind
the roar there is this silence for angels, for a secret.
Fathers are moving through sorrows of light,
they see the world as it might be and want us to
learn new dances, new songs. The kites are about
this and the silly jokes and the tree houses and the
mock boxing. They come to the family meal
and see several generations assembled. They see it in
the Christmas tree, in birthday embraces, in the hide
and seek days and the dark and stony story telling times.
Fathers want you to mend their fences, win their wars,
fall in love with their fictions, fly nearer to the sun,
discover their secret valleys, open the diary where they left off,
hold hands with their ghosts,
bury their mothers in valleys enchanted with rainbows.

VII GRADUALLY IT IS ALL UNDERSTOOD

Gradually it is all understood, at least in perceptions.
Too late and too abstract to be believed but observed
all the same. Yes; or where are we in all this? A fall of
words to accompany us, in the rooms and lanes and chancels.
A fall of words to accompany us, the winter sun surfacing
on the ordinary, surfacing on the perceived. Look; it is
about to change again! And who are we, not content
to wait for ever? Visiting the old gardens we seek
their simplicity, the order of their times now desired as
a value in itself. Other words, other voices, the days
to be filled with other people's meaning. Look at us
as we enter again the ancient, seeking the light
across traceries, ornate glass yielding the faces of
thirteenth century women who lived on the edge of death,
more in and out than fixed but held here as beautiful.
We stare at them and perhaps the distance is exalted.
In song and mime and dance their graces thrive. We hold
hands with them, we sing between their songs; seasons
are sensed and regained. Gradually this all becomes and

is made into our sense and we set out again. Our
children join us in the circle, beneath this sky of
stars. They wait with us to hear the whales. They
stroke the dead grebe and write poems about flight.
Gradually such behaviour grows abstract. The words
sing silence. The alphabets are kites, fly from
our souls. Here is blue. Here is red. Here is the
heat of the dream. Here is the silence of old letters.
In Haiti two boys run from the hill top to set
their kite above the town, the identity of town
above the living and the dead, above the entire concept of life.

X   JUST AS THE SUN BEGINS

Just as the sun begins to appear across the frost fields
the men in the asylum begin looking for their shoes
which they will never find because shoes are
not allowed in this place; shoes are no longer here.
Just as the sun reaches the courtyard and the converted
buildings and begins to dance across the tall windows
the men in the asylum begin to shuffle into the room
for food; the lumps of bread and the big brown pots
of coffee. When they eat and drink they make popping
noises because their false teeth have been taken
away and even those with teeth eat like animals.
Just as the sun enters the room of iron beds and
filthy old chairs and the unpainted walls and the
places where noise whirls all day long and there
is never any song, the soldiers arrive for their
free food and free coffee and there is booze as well.
They lock all of the patients in one room and
use some of the furniture to stoke up the fire
and then they lie out in the courtyard and sleep
it off. This happens often, at least twice a
week. When the staff ran off and only a few
volunteers remained it began and then when the place
was entirely run by the patients they came here
more and more. Free food and booze from the staff
store and even hot water whilst the fuel lasted.

When the mortar attack began they were well into
the bread and coffee and somebody had got hold of
some eggs and they were about to stuff their guts
and then the entire place was ablaze and running red.
It was as if the sun itself had lain down in each bed.

XII LETTERS LIKE MOMENTS OF LIGHT

Letters like moments of light; sometimes they never end.
You hear their voice, see the writer, enter for a moment
the place where they were written, imagined or real, time and
truth. They are more real than speech, more determined. Their
love or libel demands your mind. Only these words actually matter.
The writing is recognised like music. You know so much even by
the opening. There are refrains, there are movements and swells. But
more than tones there are territories of light that engage you
so that as you read and hear the voice you almost reply,
you begin to respond. This letter is about love and it changes you.
You are becoming something quite different. This letter is about
giving and you are deciding how to. Letters from my mother, sent on
Sundays, making Mondays. The silence of the paper. The script
that moved swiftly from chit chat to advice, to scripture.
Father's letters; badly typed, filled with instructions and condemnations
and that small change of trust. And from grandfather those long
and eloquent conversations, stories of boyhood and games. The paper
red for pirates or blue for air balloons or green for forests.
And the love letters; to and from America, to and from dreams,
small songs to conquer distance, jokes to juggle the orthodoxy,
the thin air-mail paper to carry the full weight of adoration.
And then my letters to daughters, the drawings and rhymes;
and letters that were final letters, the meanings that
went off the page, the letters that simply did not say;
the letters that we keep from the dead. In the sentence
of summer nights I sometimes read these in my mind.
Letters in the head. The voice still there. The face
of the voice. The speaker calm now. All that has
been said beyond the vocabulary of this world. Another
alphabet that speaks when the other songs are silenced.

XIV NOW, VERY GENTLY, THE MAID IS RUNNING ACROSS THE LAWN

Now, very gently, the maid is running across the lawn
that has become tufted and wild. There used to be tennis
and croquet here and bowls but then the gardener joined the
army. Now there are poppies and thistles and rabbits and
the bough that fell from the cedar lies like a ruined
boat between what was a line of rose beds and the ha ha.
Today I am three years old and the deckchair has begun
to collapse and it is slowly locking in my left hand thumb.
As I scream I can see the maid moving across the lawn
and there are rooks overhead and somewhere beyond the scream
there is the sound of the brass dinner gong. It comes from
the house, from the hall, from the silent interior where
the grandfather clock whispers each second. Very gently
now the maid is running across my screams and her eyes
hold me as if I were a fallen bird and there was a
hole in the sky. She attacks the deckchair as if it
were a monster crab and cradles me to her chest.
I can smell her now. A mixture of furniture polish
and potatoes rises from her arms. I can see the freckles
on her forehead as she carries me across the ocean of
tufted lawn where the dead birds rot, past the
Edwardian summerhouse and into the glebeland where
each cow ruminates on the eternity of meadows.
The dinner gong is out of hearing now. The sound
has gone out because we are now surrounded by
forest. In the forest you can begin to believe
in angels again and other people's alphabets don't
get in the way and the paths are those you make
yourself and the only stories are of owls and stars
and those you invent before the police arrive on bicycles.

XV OPEN THIS LETTER; IT MIGHT SAY SOMETHING

Open this letter; it might say something that we could call
a something, not merely a message back. Today and every
day millions of words fixed into envelopes and sent through
dazzling densities when the telephone or e-mail or fax

might do. But apparently this does not do. It is the paper
and the hand and the space to be that we believe in,
that we yield to, that we most trust. I can see
the poet Frank Kuppner getting ready for another
day of letters, whispering to him, making his day. And
when they do not arrive one wonders if they will ever be
sent. In a drawer somewhere I still keep my father's
and my mother's last letters. His was telling me what to
do, formulating a family re-union and setting up his
own scenario as usual. Mother's was a gentle letting
go whilst she could still remember who I was and didn't
yet address me as 'that gentleman' or 'our visitor'
or 'Mister who ever you are'. The
letters gradually collapsed, her pen began to trail,
the sentences got shorter, the letters became single paragraphs
and then simply notes and then they didn't
exist at the start of a day. Open this letter;
it needs to become its voice, it needs to tell
us, it needs to speak. And between what will be
preliminary and casual and no more than this and that
there will sometimes be signals of vital news,
news that goes beyond the telling, a truth
that must get through. It is about us and
our world and what we mean to make it. It is
a statement made against pain and rumour.
It is saying what we are actually doing here.

XVIII REMEMBER THE NIGHT THEY CAME
TO TAKE THE NUMBERS AWAY

Remember the night they came to take the numbers away;
we were dreaming in stars and the schoolroom was song
but they took the teacher out and shot him into dark.
Remember the night they came to take the alphabet away;
we were in the church with angels and other souls
but they took the priest away and took out his vision.
Remember the night they came to take our lives away;
we were in the forest and could see them from the edge
as they set fire to the women and silenced the men.

From that day we became the people of the forest
and drew out our existence beneath ancient canopies
even when our minds walked down to the ruins of homes.
We all did that a bit, a walk in the head down to
the place where the church had been and the school
field and we saw the swing with birds on it and
in the street we could still see our old world.
In our heads we kept the numbers safe and the language
safe and the idea of village secure even when the
snow filled up to the sky and there was only silence.
And over and over we buried the remains of the women
and filled the silent places of these men with songs
and whistling and the gasp of air as they swung down
the axe in the yard in the old days of autumn .
Now our children skip to different songs and we have
made a place in their minds that is set in green.
The school is between these trees and the church
is beneath those boughs and the angels come from
those limbs. And the God is beyond the trees
and the animals and the sunrays and the rain,
the snow. The God still keeps flying between dreams and belief.

XIX SO ONCE WE HAVE DECIDED

So once we have decided that we are all living
in the sky, we are certain of this, definitions are
changed once and for all. There is no other view. This
is the way to be. It's all understood and what we once
regarded as permanent is but the brushwork of dreams.
Where do we go from here? Indeed. And where are we
to establish ourselves in sky? The obsolete items are
falling through space along with planets and atoms and
what we have achieved is total access. There is
no longer need to establish a God or sense of
HIM. There is no setting out from here. Notion
upon notion has become particle. Sleep and dancing
is necessary still, of course, and the ability to
express the inexpressible. Once there were trees and
tracks between and the movement of humans and their

quest for ideas. Once there were zoos and cathedrals
and other institutions that made a meaning within.
Now we can concentrate on what really matters
but it never actually occurs. The fact is that
fact is fiction and what we regarded as truth was
always a translation. The angels are out on
the fields of eternity again and who are we
to interpret their wisdoms? What we get is
the initial, the primary, the idea before
it has found a voice or hand or action.
What does it mean for the past, you ask?
Well, who are you and would you hear us even
if we did spill the beans? Now all life
is pure energy, a voice before it has said.
Living in the sky, we are certain of this.

XXII   VERY SLOWLY MY GRANDMOTHER IS FALLING TO BITS

Very slowly my grandmother is falling to bits.
She used to sit in the wooden armchair and shut
tight her eyes consuming hot tea. There were always
two biscuits. She used to give us dark chocolate
and her room smelt of lavender fields, old wood, bibles.
Today she is slowly falling to bits, falling from pillow
calm and prayer peace through a tangle of sheets
to the ornate carpet and its scatter of magazines.
Slowly, too, the rooks are wheeling about
their nests, above the coppice where we hide between
our necessary games. Now my mother is looking in
to discover her splayed across the floor as if she had
slipped from a dream of angels, caught between one
alleluia and another leap of psalms. Gently the
afternoon sun is curtained out, the outside world shut
out, the bedroom becoming a monument. When they
lifted her back into bed grandmother's face began to
shrink until all that was left was her nose.
Gently now my father sits in this room to pray.
Each word cascades through chancels of memory,

her voice within his voice, psalm upon psalm
in this threnody of faith. Each day we enter
to replace the flowers. We give up games for a
week. We see our father weep. After the funeral
he sits in the room and reads her diary. We
look up from the garden and know that he is there. Gently
now the owl, the stars, the garden paths, even
the toys; changed. At night our father lights
a candle in the room and I dream of grandmother
walking into the coppice surrounded by owls.

XXV   YES, WE WRITE POETRY; WHAT DO YOU WRITE?

Yes, we write poetry; what do you write?
And sometimes we read it between living and dreams,
and sometimes we find other people to read it to, and
sometimes we meet somebody who quotes back a line or two
from a life we left years ago, and sometimes there is a
line that races beyond our lives and catches us at stages.
Yes, we write it because it keeps coming, prompting, essential,
a wolf howl in the soul until we hunt down the impulse
and create the new thing; and what do you do? Where are
your secret fields and discovered pathways and wild toys?
Where are your voices from the wings and small rooms of the
imagination and other lives? Between the funerals of great
aunts and procession of gangsters a vision of lilacs. Between
the silence of Quaker meetings and the surges on football
terraces three nuns consuming ice cream. Between my
grandfather's sermons and the bishop's requests for jazz
an image of Elgar at the race track. And somewhere
between Mostar and Kosovo the mothers who sleep
beyond the dawn, the church bells, the sirens, the
roar of falling buildings, the scream of homes bleeding
to death, the silence of playgrounds. In Spain
the funeral party still makes its way through the
narrow streets with enormous wreaths and the women
with giant handbags. The priest waits for
them and the choirboys stare as the San Miguel
beer truck crashes into the coffin, into the wreaths,

into the handbags, into the prayers written in heads,
into the speeches, into the memories of gardens and family meals,
into the late afternoon sun like a blazing drum.

XXVI   ZENNOR LIGHT

Zennor light; across Chysauster, Men-an-tol, the
villages and tombs, from Carn Naun Point to Gurnard's Head,
the light falling like fleece. And in November the homes like night
nests, gripping between bare green, slate sheen, a granite God.
Ridges of lichen rock, sea pink ripple, crests and troughs of winter light,
broken tides of ancient psalms. Each home wound in its wind skin,
its own tide, Godrevy Light waiting for its schooners, a red sun in
September, a green sun in May. And in St. Ives Alfred Wallis escaping
the Devil who mutters down the chimney, sends the kids to hurl abuse,
escaping the radio voices, mechanical things, covering up his pictures on
the Sabbath. On bits of board, cups, bellows, trays, his white and
green maps, his grey and brown tides, to capture what used to be
before the fishing died, before The Evil came, to deny the stench
of loneliness, the loss, the hollow, to give each boat its soul again,
to give us origins and safe harbours past the religious thing and echoes
and dreams; for company, for peace, for the real life to come again.
Alfred Wallis searching for the perfect surface again, painting
upon belief, the faith that could dance, the feel of belief.
Granite gives us paths in August. Cradled in sea surge
the Zennor bell wind-gusting God, His belly stuffed with gulls and rope,
His miracles hauled across rock, His text hailed by mermaids,
His saints hidden beneath circles of stone. At Ding Dong
the clouds chase angels across the fields, set the geese running
like crazy nuns, rattle the hunched hedgerows near a holy well.
Nettle dark, cold as dead bone, hard as bell, the water
waits for secrets, truths, vows, treasons. Each month a man comes
here with a prayer scratched on a piece of card. Sometimes it is a
poem. Sometimes it is a hymn. He ties it to the nearest branch
before retreating down a track that is forever vanishing.

from *Bosnia*

Bosnia

So, let's express it as it is. What we thought was ours
we inherited, used, attributed but never owned. This
paper, these texts; these assurances, metaphors, prayers even.
These images, expressions, interpretations; always translated
on the other side of faith. A yield of other people's histories,
abstracts, tirades and fictions; even our songs borrowed from
other tribes. We have been educated by foreign agendas.

Looking across the valley I thought I could see more villages
burning. Or was it the procession of priests coming down from
evening services? Or was it a signal for me to set fire to
my neighbour's home, burning their vision into the ground?
Or was this merely another haunting as we woke up to
hear the silence chilling; not a scream, not a dog
yelping, not the trundling of hundreds of cars as
civilians make their escape, flee to another life?
Looking across the valley I thought then that I could
see my mother and father many years ago, so long
it might as well be centuries; stopping to look back,
to search, to offer me a place in their sad procession,
ready to make room for my dreams, my terrors, my toys.

So, let's express it as it is. You see this photograph.
You see this boy and the trees and the edge of a house.
Is it me? Is it my father? Who held the camera?
And what is that flying in the distant sky?
Looking across the valley I thought I could hear
their singing; not old women or priests
but men lost to us in the midst of secret camps.

But there is no place for singing now. All songs
became war signals, all music mosaics of mutilation;
whispers travel where soldiers may not march, a letter
is a life, a woman in an orchard becomes a flag. We

stare out from fragile sanctuaries watching the land change
sides. We have no names for this place. Secret maps are
folded in the head. Dismembering is an act of logistics.

There is no blood in a pencil but life blood. So we sit
reading newspapers that are two years old or we play the
retelling game; our heroes all die, the gods deceive,
nobody discovers the distant islands and the lovers
only remained together for a few days after 'THE END'.

Looking across the valley one thinks of all the others
who might be looking back. They also have packed bags
hidden and ready. They also have made their farewell speeches
yet expect to survive. The trees hide us in from each other
and the foliage of fear. We have learnt so much about
distances; between what we once said and what we now
mean, between the idea of days and our current occupations,
between a neighbour's wave and a stranger on the horizon,
between the story told by the teacher and the truth
told over the telephone. When the letters get through
we sometimes wait for a few hours or even a day or two
before unfolding them; separate, delineate, acknowledge
precisions, yield to judgements. One day we received
a photograph from Cologne. The words were from
people we recognised but the truths on their faces
were foreign. They looked like clips from a movie.
They looked like participants in a stage play.

So, once again, we intrude on reality and act out
small incidents of normalcy. Looking cross the valley
we have all seen strangers occupying a home where once
we knew the occupants, their fields, their animals.
We imagine what they have hidden in their hearts. We
don't know where they are anymore. And the people who have
taken over must be aware of those formerly there, trying
to get a grip, occupying, taking over, invading.
There are days when we have taken shelter and coming
back we had expected to recognise no-one. We are
always surprised that anything at all remains. When

the planes fly over, when there is gunfire, when there
are voices, when there are flames again, when a strange
dog appears in the garden, when a soldier runs past,
when a letter is handed over, when we take the words
off the page, when we stare at a photograph album,
when the juice of the apple is excellent, when the
smell of the bread is beautiful, when the lines of a
poem or a story rekindle, when we are lifted by
the vision of stars at night, when we hear a man
calling to his cows, when we are looking across the
valley and we can see the faces of people we know
facing us back then we know that we are no
longer helpless, that we might begin the language
again, begin to order the words again, begin
to revive the possibility, looking across the valley
because we are still here, looking right across,
aware that we are all now waving back at ourselves.

from *Conversations Before the End of Time*

The Fiction Enters

The fiction enters. In the midst of reality
when survival strategies obsess
a notion invades offering assurances, the powerhouse
of poetry dumps something dazzling in your mind
and away you go; courageous, careless, determined to see
the story through, aware that one has been taken over.
Let the laundry rot. The garden is a jungle anyway.
The 'phone can speak to itself and now that the word
is wired let's appoint the machines as managers.
Whilst the toothpaste departs, the letter box sighs,
the Hoover hovers, the hosepipe heads towards lupins,
your mind seizes on stories, rhymes, myths, riddles;
the fiction of oneself spawning between other people's
lives and lies, a vocabulary of values networking
as you recover from dreams, stroll towards the

summerhouse, raise the glass, ripple the diary,
enter the novel, catch a phrase from the radio play,
listen to Hitler, hear suddenly your father's voice
as you remove cobweb from the croquet set.

Hide and Seek for Kenneth Koch

It is a fact that when somebody is speaking of this
there are others who will be speaking of that;
these people carefully erect a wall whilst others
have plans to remove a wall stone by stone;
those who decide to let the end of the garden
go wild might find others just over the fence
about to design new beds, trim the thicket,
roll out a tennis court, clip the yew.
For every person who leaps forward somebody
whispers 'hold back'. For every dreamer there
is a solitary individual who says 'all fantasy
is futile'. For every old lady who sits with her
dentures biting a scowl there is another old
one who keeps lusting for her husband's bum;
'a little loaf, a small brown loaf, oven warm'.
It is a fact. For every person. The fiction and the
fact dancing across midsummer lawns.

Not Dancing in Letterkenny

Because he could not dance
he walked across the hall
in the midst of dancers
steered by my smiling mother
who made it seem like dancing.

In his head dancing was the arrival
of a magnificent idea, a sudden truth,
or the sunsets in Cornwall
or swimming along the track of gold,
bathing in diamonds.

At Letterkenny there was also a
dance on the beach one evening.
He knew exactly what to do when
the band started up
so he strolled out alone.

Between the sea and the torches
he knew how to do it;
you are what the music makes you,
dancing now.

A View of the World

Look, I am closing all the doors
and saying 'not now' to the light
in the orchard trees and am saying
'no' to the dancing children;

and even the words I have written
begin to bend down and not to challenge
and the music belongs somewhere else:

and the terror of it is not possible,
the option is not possible, the gesture that
I have witnessed in other men appears false;

and between the time of day and a time of night
the kites of childhood fly again, above all the
houses and remembered rooms;

above all the schools and the serious teachers,
above all the churches and the lumpy angels,
above all the parks where secrets floated
and soldiers strolled;

above what the grandparents never said,
above where the owl crashed into the tree house,
above where a view of the world runs out of light.

Conversations Before the End of Time

Conversations before the end of time, before
we forget how to speak and the silences become nests, before
the urban myths become realities and not tests of truth, before
the hidden alphabets of men collapse in sodden vanities, before
the priest gets so used to miracles he forgets the necessity of whispers, before
poets who have danced all night return to their words and the secrets of
    gardens.

Rust Soup

When I was wanting to write the book about seasons
tramps kept coming into it and sitting in the driveways to large houses.
When I was wanting to write the book about tramps
priests kept chanting in the places where the tramps should have been.
When I was wanting to write a book about priests
uncles and aunties kept asking me what I wanted to be
and when I told them I wanted to be a writer and write books
about seasons and tramps and priests they pleaded with me
to include something about their own lives,
where hours and hours were spent
waiting to become uncles and aunts
bobbing about in the storms of life in inadequate boats

with umbrellas that blew inside out
and suppers that turned into rust soup.

In the Meantime

In the meantime
what we receive is other peoples texts, dreamtimes,
trading in fables. Exactly where we are is somewhere
between the loss of childhood and the discovery of invented Edens.
Fighting for an identity all these years. Shoving our parents over
clifftops even as we adore them. Returning to sacred areas where
winter sun is all we seek, retreating to sacred stones and
conversations held on the edge. Every time the poem is written a
new song changes the singer and only the listener knows it is not new.
Discovering the old, discoursing between the grass and bones and there
is always that fond light that surpasses storm and the silence
of the night room when nothing can truly be said and meant.
Hallo. Are you the person setting out or settling for less or are you
the person who constantly returns? Goodbye then. Are you the self
who sets down these messages and provides provisional answers and lets
a psalm slip when all we had meant was a rather elaborate joke?
There in the hallway mirror is my mother still scolding me
for ruining the bulbs in what I had seen as the heroic jungle.
And there are the texts that I did not read in the school
library where the books ticked, waited, decorated, upheld.
And there is the orchard still crowded with voices as we
pick the apples, pull the rotten ladder out of white grass,
rescue the chinese geese from the fire, wait for the aconites.
Now you can hear skipping songs from the playground
and somebody has a radio on in one of the almshouses. Perhaps we will
    all die
because of Cuba. In the late afternoon light the white horse becomes a
    unicorn again
and what the radio does not say is canticle, chorus, convulsions of angels.
Hallo again. Do you see me returning and what should
we say of the years in between? Nobody dances like Sonia in the winter

palace before the soldiers arrive and the band becomes blood. When the palace
was set on fire all the windows popped as though ghosts burst through them.
The trees were also on fire as the patients from the asylum gathered as if
to sing and in each nest a vesper gently boiled. In the playroom
we sit and cut up images from magazines. Here is a girl with a dancing bear.
Here is a hotel with blue curtains. Here are the tennis courts in moonlight.

And in each image we cut up the words that must have existed. We
also invent words to occupy the images, the rooms that cannot be, the
names for children who skate on the huge lake, small speech bubbles
for the factory workers in Islington, names for the soldiers who dance
in the winter palace and dig their spurs into the grand piano shine.
From the top bedrooms where once servants wept for entire lifetimes you
can look across the formal gardens, the lawns, the parks, the orchards, the forests
for hundreds of years. There also is the ruin of the plague village. There also
is the barn where spies were hung. And there is the hill where a maid
gave birth whilst flying a kite. Today sixty hot air balloons are
about to rise and fly above this scene of limited significance. In the meantime we
return to our memories and anecdotes and Press Cuttings and e mail and website
scenarios that urge us to compete. In the meantime I read of beasts and barricades and
how the water is killing us all. The Irish are still fighting
their seven hundred year war.
In a house in Tipperary a cousin walks his acres the axe swinging by his side.
The house is slipping into a dotage of cats. The drive smells of cats. The
private chapel reeks of cats. There is a dead cat beneath every tree. It was
I think the household of Borodin that was dominated by His Grace The Cat.
In a house in Tipperary a cousin begins each evening with a strict piano piece
dedicated to the timelessness of cats. You can hear his playing from the main
gate which still carries scars of the rebellion. The remaining trees on the old
estate adjust their sails. Mad captains, high winds.

The Ghost Terraces

In one's head the familiar fictions of the dead.
Great Uncle Reggie whose son was lost at sea
now marooned in tea rooms, whispering hallways
where the servants have changed from black to white.
His wife; where did he put her and what is she saying
to perfect strangers? Vicars and doctors all speak alike
and sometimes one counts the years by counting the trees. Wind
has taken over their lives and summer days are stripping away.
They dress as if a great event awaited them. They
wait for letters and postcards of cathedrals caught in shafts
of sun. Their greatest fear is the death of Cook. Last
year a rat ran in through the scullery door. The gardener
got plastered and drove the mower over the ha-ha. In the
front hall a fox stood totally still as Uncle Reggie
applauded. He thought it brought a message, good news.

My Sister is Flying

My sister is flying again. She does
this sometimes to annoy the words. Or is

it that the silences are falling and she can
get in between before the words return?

Anyway, she is once again flying to
and fro between the Victorian summer house

and the garden shed that is almost hidden
in the yew tree, the green density.

We, of course, go about our doing
that and this, the growing and cutting

that becomes a garden. She on the
other hand flies between the bird

feeder and the squirrel run and the
wind sock shaped like an old hag.

It is Easter time and we have hung
the plastic eggs on the silver birch boughs

yet again. This means that when she flies
there are several obstacles that she needs to avoid

but mostly it is the words, the speech, that
is so utterly conventional and yet essential.

The Magician Prepares Afternoon Tea

After the letters have been heard again
and talk of gifts lost or never received
and walks down the imagined garden path
and the eternal voices of children,
the Magician once again elevates the
tea table, the cake on its plate, the pot
and the jug and we wait now for other
wisdoms from the man in the black suit.
What it is to live between the hills
and the greenness of daylight. What
it is to have such faith. And after
the tea more talk and then a period
of silence. And after the silence
waiting to see what he does with
the remains of his trick. Who will
come to clear the tea things;
perhaps an angel? Or will it be
something left in the mind, lost
in time, claimed by the night,
gently lifted into clouds of moon?

Dear Whatever

Dear Whatever Your Name Is;
when your letter arrived I was basking in the Goldberg Variations
and the letter box was on fire.
As the music assembled its whatever I began to think of
the pianist with his feet stuck into Kleenex boxes; or
was that another genius who lost his grip here and entered there
and lived between this ecstasy and that threat and lost his ability
to chill; Howard whoever you are or were?
When your words arrived I was in fact in bed and the sound of the postman
entered a dream about making music and I was about to enter the library
to enquire about who it was who invented the piano because we all know
who invented manholes and umbrellas and windmills and barbed wire
    but not
who began to begin the piano, mother of all instruments.
And your letter was such a success. I too had children who disappeared into
adults leaving their toys in the attic, their books in the garage. And
who was that woman they invented and talked to and invited to tea and
when they came home from school in the summer term who was she who
waited for them at the bottom of the lawn; a Mrs. Cotterbee.
Perhaps you know her. She does certain words and has invented countries
like Afreekar and Jamaiker and Bustin. I liked
the bit about the dog and its dreaming on the rug and what you
said to the vicar when he said there was no room in heaven
for pets. I liked the way you dealt with Egon Ronay's
Cellnet Guide when all you wanted was a room with a view
of a real sea and a real harbour and a real peal of bells.
Dear Whatever Your Name Is; yes, I received your letter
but it had been mislaid, delayed, lost in the toss of
time. I am not sure of who. I am not sure of what.
It was not meant for me and yet. It was not sent to
be. And yet. And now I am here sending this to you when
I don't in fact even know your name as the writing looked like
lice or ruined lace and only the address was clear.
The vicar has just driven past and when the piano tuner comes
I will make him play for his coffee and cake and this and that
will enter my day as it always does and you and I will have
exchanged greetings across the coldness of winter whispers.

Beautiful Ruins

Listen.
Into our silence comes sleep.
Again we weep autumns but
then bells tell us legends.
Atonements slumber in
winter gardens and all we saw
as truths became parables.
Look at us dancing
between what we meant
and what our words said.
And when we looked towards
the ancient all we heard was
God's laughter in beautiful
ruins. Hey.

Coming Into a Blue Room

Coming into a blue room,
the stare of time and one's recognition of it.
There is no immediate answer although one does
not mind the question. Look at me. Look at
us all. Observe our days. The table waits for
the meal. The mirror waits for its faces. The clock
stands up for time and declarations and light
dances from shadow to shade.
It is early, it is late; it makes no difference
because it has all been written down in somebody's
fictions already. These are the words that did it.
These are the sentences that told. In the blue room
the flowers become white, the silences become white,
laughter patterns like small butterflies. From a
window I can see myself looking out and looking
in. I wave and my mother waves back. She waves
and a small boy smiles. All he can think of is kites.

Grandfather's Letters

He puts the words down, down deliberately,
almost as if drawing, so that we will want to
explore them, fathom, revel in the wriggle and squiggle,
the plucking of punctuation to make a point, capital
letters like soldiers at attention, the 'T's shaped like trees,
and the paper so carefully selected, deep red or green or that
bird's egg blue, to draw special attention, to hold the mind,
to make us listen to his fun, his seriousness, so that we might
see him at his desk in his last years, his kindly light to remain.
He puts the words down, down in our minds on the jolly paper,
his notions of what we may like and understand, his stories,
sometimes a message for mother, often a mention of Mr. Churchill
or The Queen, often an account of that day in the garden,
discovering a toad or a butterfly, a dead bird found behind
the log box, once the odour of foxes. He puts down these words
and the years will come and cover him with grass and snow and prayers.
I wait my turn now, to begin such things. To write such words.
To put them down in my own measure. The red of robins.
The green of February lawns. The brilliant eggshell blue.
And squiggles, elegant as feathers. A kindly light passed on.

Two Old Ladies

Two old ladies are dancing on the main lawn.
Mr. Snow is hiding newspapers again. Several patients
are shuffling back from the chapel. God is out.

Two old ladies are dancing on the main lawn;
long after the record player has been put away.
For supper there were sausages and ice cream.

Two old ladies are dancing on the main lawn.
Everyone is meant to be in bed. The television was
as crazy as ever. Rachel is still screaming.

Two old ladies are dancing on the main lawn.
When all the lights go out the green of August
gently pools with images of childhood games.

We often dressed up and walked through the garden
arm in arm or pretended that we were at funerals,
or that two old ladies might be dancing on the main
lawn.

Histories

Their voices never quite depart. Our minds
return and return, some places always accompanying;
playrooms, tree houses, roof spaces, under the stairs
where the stench of umbrellas hung. And in the spare
bedroom there was a silence of afternoon sunshine, a never
hurrying whisper of great aunts who arrived with messages
and other people's stories and ancient texts in their heads,
who took 'naps' after lunch, their dreams draped like lace
over established vistas, their God nestling in a hat box and
smelling of candles. When they departed the room returned to
its lilt; the maid found some Christian token by the bed,
the pillows retained that odour of stale mint. It was as if
their prayers were still there, folded for eternity, small traces
and hints at wit, biscuit thin. Then Uncle William came, suffering
still from shell shock. He always held his hands behind his back
bracing his shoulders. His dentures clicked. We never quite knew when
his jokes ended unless he added 'and that was that, you understand'.
When he had his stroke his dentures broke and he went rigid as a pole.
His hands went yellow, locked by his sides, thumbs sticking out
as if on parade, which of course he was. He could see God on a white
charger coming towards him, all the soldiers standing to attention,
all the poppies bobbing, all those men he'd known in the trenches
stiffly saluting, all the questions and the answers falling into place,
all the meanings meaning, 'and that was that, you understand'.

Woman in Her Orchard, Vitez. Bosnia.

The pears are ready. If she does not pick them soon
frost will kill, they will not be fit to eat;
another irony in a town where once
everyone was proud of their gardens.

The pears are ready. She has decided to go out.
She will pick as many as she can before retreating
to the darkness of the house, the photographs and letters
telling her of the old life.

She tugs on the old coat. She walks through tall grass
and smells the bark of trees, the large fruits;
she feels the firmness of each pear, its wholeness,
its silence.

Her neighbour is at work now. She can hear him
and his gun. His noise wings over her like a monstrous bird
its wings on fire.

She swiftly escapes to the deep interior of the house
hiding her basket of fruit. Entering the kitchen
she hears the voices of her men
calling from distant fields.

Border Country. Former Yugoslavia

'There is nothing one man will not do to another.'
    Carolyn Fouché

Returning after the experience of war
they enter the house that has been in
their minds for three years. They walk
the path, arrive at the door, enter a ruin.
They cross rubble seeking a place. They approach
the door that was hacked and burnt. They

enter rooms that had been on fire. Look;
there is the small library, there is the table
where they gather to eat, there is the mirror.
All the pages flew loose in flames. The old
man was crucified on the table. They all ran
through the mirror and passed across to another
planet. Listen; here is a cupboard of
screams, here is a drawer of curses;
can you hear the corner sobbing?
When they have been back a few days
they begin to notice the neighbour again.
He is staring across. He can
never forget that they were all dead.
Meanwhile, water, food,
possibly words.

In Fields of Ancient Light

It was always known that they would do this;
initially the sniper picking on the women as they made their way
early in the morning. Later total bombardment, the ruin itself
in flames. Then, gradually, even the ruin removed so that there would
be nothing left to see. Weeds, grass, in time a vehicle parked there.
No sign to survive.

In their heads beyond the horror, beyond what they had endured,
the old women who stored the symbols, the songs, the statements
made against ruin and revenge. And some had even saved a few
vital treasures; a piece of glass, a fragment of carving, an image
of the divine, a scrap of text. To be hidden, to be brought out
in front of the most trusted.

In one village, in the mountains, rumours of ruin and rape
compelled them to act ahead of tragedy. Even if they were
finally to be found out they must do this now. Mostly alone,
often at night or in fields of ancient light at dawn they
took their treasures and buried them wrapped in sacking or plastic;
the fragile, the blessed, the ornate.

In one village, in winter, even the bells,
hidden in ancient earth; their silence, their trust.

Three Men are Carrying Geese

Three men are carrying geese across a field of sun.
Meanwhile the children must learn not to lie and how to
untie the confusions of life. The tourists who have come here
explore the park and marvel at the castle gates. Six miles
away two rivers meet and both change their name.

Three men are carrying geese across this sunny field.
Meanwhile the teachers must learn how to confuse the children
who always attend. Soldiers let the tourists get within a hundred
yards of the secret places. In a turret three men are discussing
how to change the face of war.

Three men are carrying geese across a field of sunset.
Their wives and their children are waiting for them to return.
It has taken a lifetime to get this far. Now that they
are no longer soldiers they can talk to strangers but
there are none. They have even forgotten the names of flowers.

Three men are carrying geese across an evening field.
Every mile they walk reminds them of their families.
They look out for strangers to help them find their way.
There used to be a river and a school and a castle and
a church and a god. There used to be a house and a door

just here.

After Occupation

Before the soldiers arrive
we take the library books and hide them
in the woods, in windmills, in asylums.

When the soldiers are occupying
they speak of art and poetry and between
the dances they recite.

When the soldiers depart
we wait, surrounded by ruins;
some of the hiding places are
now in a foreign country.

We stand up and open our mouths
and we all applaud the rush
of silence.

We can't even find the keys
to our fields.

A

A man is running and his house is on fire
and we are in our gardens
using the words we always sing.

A man is running and his house and his dog are on fire
and we say enter our house
and we will let you enter our dance.

A man is running and his house and his dog and his children are on fire
and we say hear our prayers and here
is a hymn so sit down and quiet.

A man is running and his house and his dog and his children and his bed
are on fire are on fire
and the birds are burning also and the small church by the lake
and the grandfather clock and the place where he hid his letters;

and we are saying come in and dance the prayer with us
and say the songs that we all make true
and we will share our sounds and give you our silences
and so you will be so still.

A man is running in the stillness of the house
and in the silence of the hurt dog
and in the sounding of the children
and in the doing of the garden;

and we are all immortal in his intent
and we are all now running in his meaning
and we are all now becoming in his words.

His silence sits on the mantel with the flowers,
his silence occupies a new place at the table,
his silence ascends the stairs to the little bedroom,
his silence rattles in the early morning bathroom.

His silence occupies our house
and will and will

and will.

Fathers

In night dreams, in folded rooms, the children
see their fathers beneath apple boughs and stars.
Their wardrobes have the odour of pullovers and blazers,
their jokes are out of sync, too bright, bouncy

as school jellies. But they can still mend punctures,
polish an apple, untie the demon knots, and when
the kites come out they are air controllers, the eagles
move aside, the wind complies. In church on Sundays
they read the Lessons as if their lives depended on it;
the rhythm of necessities and taut mythologies, the
poetry of chosen tribes. And in the night dreams,
in folded rooms, when the mothers have closed the doors,
it is the fathers who are there with conkers and marbles,
train sets and the small coins hidden in smiles.

Putting the Fathers Out

Some have done this early on. It seems good.
For others it is the longest struggle. Neither earth
nor flame properly separate, shield, let loose.
The years return the words, the voices, the closest
ghost who enters each festival, never forgets.
We know what we have to do. Bury the words in
deep forests, sing louder than the intruder, believe
in the future and stop fumbling for the past;
and yet and yet. In fearing to betray do we
betray ourselves? What do we hold on to?
At this desk his paperweight, his ruler, his
armchair. Somewhere the last letter, folded
over, the eccentric typing, the assured scrawl.
The face that faces you back when you weren't
even looking, weren't even listening. The children
who have already stuffed the roof space and
garage with their own treasures, totems, toys.

Wolf Mother Never

The wolf is always there, even when the field is safe
and the voice of your mother is calling your name.
Even when you can see her and run towards her face
because that is the part of her you never forget.
Even when the prayers fail to come and the old
tricks don't work and everything in the letters lies damp
and ruined. Even when the voices are solid and real.
The wolf is always between the trees and between
the houses and between the pretty views and between
the laughter. The wolf hides in the parcel
that one day could be opened. The wolf sits
inside the shadow of the grandfather clock
waiting to strike thirteen. And you go on
and on across the field and across the world
seeing the face of your mother in windows
and mirrors and pictures and drawings and other
people's photograph collections and on videos
and in magazines and in postcards. All
of your life you see her and run towards
her face because that is the part of her
that you never forget. Never.

Small Incidents in Large English Gardens

The man waits for the child to stop hitting him on the head.
When the hose is turned on the grandmother heads for the toilet.
Deadheading the roses waits to be done.
Bowling waits to take place. The bowls are no longer stored in a case.
They are stuffed into a Waitrose bag in the summerhouse.
From someone else's tennis courts we hear effete screeches.
Edwardian windows look out on sepia visions.
The long driveways have been built on for years now.
When it is time for tea you have to make it yourself.
Down by the river they are raising a hot air balloon.

We will not look up. We will wait for the six o'clock news
to inform us what has become of dragonflies. A dunnock
takes a dust bath where we buried dear Victor only last year.

Sheds

Odour of great escapes, screw top jars, tobacco tins,
dead dog. A ladder going nowhere; tuckbox a tool store.
Wire coils and ripples of rope; signals of unfinished business.
Even in winter a hint of late summer, the girlie calendar
stroked by spiders; smell of apples and cycle tyres; an old radio
dedicated to maiden overs and occasional scores.
And the man, coming here like a bullied boy, to let
the natural dust gather, to finger through magazines or
release a stubborn cry. Coming here to remember clocks
and bells and slow lanes, a woman's simple questions.
Once the dog came here, listening for mice.
Once the perfections of peace percolated here.
Now, in winter, with the three bar fire,
he bends into a day dream,
he originates like Noah.

Marching Off the Map

When you did not hear us, when we did not talk to you,
the edge of all things transcended,
were we truly the floating souls of previous dreams
or explorers beyond the possible?

To have declared our dares, to have jumped over the
floodlit notions, to have uncoded every conformity
and split the hairs of the LAWS; and
not a prankster in sight!

There were no postcards. At night we waited for natives.
Silence lay in our minds like a dead angel. And we
all began to sing a jolly song.

Now we float, transcending tragedy, beyond the
filth of guilt. Dreaming of stars and trees
and the ancient temptations.

Easter Garden

At Easter it all begins again. My daughters
still insist on hunting for eggs and when it rains
we hide the chocolates inside the house, between books,
on the mantel, on ledges, at the base of the grandfather clock.
Now we open the windows and light enters our minds again
and I can see my parents standing by the lily pond waiting
for the frogs. Their spawn floats like an old lady's hairnet
as the dog circles its tail and sniffs at the mown grass.
And somewhere still the previous owners are here and the people
before them right back to the blind woman who must have
sensed all this, becoming it, leaving something here. We all
collect here, old men gardening, young children hiding,
the elegant tennis players, the present and the past,
folded into the being of a garden in this living light.

from *The Man Who Thought That He Was*

The Man Who Thought That He Was

THE MAN WHO THOUGHT THAT HE
WAS BACKGROUND MUSIC

You do not hear me although I seldom cease speaking
and what I become is so distant it is a whisper. You
do not respond and whatever mood I adopt I am half
way off, out of focus, lost in a world of shades. I am
the blues forgotten, the ripple of Liszt, the musak man
and yet I yearn for boogy nights and massive nightmusik and
a dance to make your knees weak. Perhaps there is
a time when you need me, lean into my gestures, smile at
the limp eloquence of my forgetfulness. You can do without me.
You can roll on a drum and murder me with sleep. I am the
sound of empty rooms, deserted lounges, lost movements and the
gradualness of glass. I repeat myself. I begin all over again.
Turned down or off. You never miss me until I am gone.

THE MAN WHO THOUGHT THAT HE
WAS A SECRET ALPHABET

Not that anyone will understand, the need I mean.
Talk straight, look you in the eye, take it on the chin;
I'd rather know than not be told; sticks and stones and.
Language as gristle. Language as the eyes in the back of the facts
and let's not forget the silence of the gods, the deepness of what
is not expressed, or if it is is seldom heard, or if it is not rarely
understood. What level of silence are we referring to here? What
is the sound of the spirit? I go out, I go in. Talking to
myself again I keep strictly off the facts. The words I
want to hear hum to a different drum and when all is said
and done there is nothing but this secret vocabulary to replace
the white of bone, the core of stone. I am what I say.
I say, I say; did you hear the one about? About what?

THE MAN WHO THOUGHT THAT HE WAS A PAPER BAG

Snug. Defined by size. No distortions when
I go about my business. There are many ways of covering up
and containing. There are even more ways of protecting.
In a world of foul and filth what it is to be so simple.
Even the Universal Declaration of Human Rights has its bag
and the Bible and the girlie mag. Assisting in the fight against fluff,
I wait, take my turn, wait to be picked up and made proper
use of. Only the slightest noise. The only thing I fear is the
bunch of kids, wet lips and hot air and suddenly I'm filling up
ready to explode. Shredded. Litter.
I am here to carry, to conceal, to hold on to essentials
in a universe that is breaking up, denying its customs.
A secret. A gift. A message. Back to basics.

THE MAN WHO THOUGHT THAT HE WAS AN EEL

Three in the morning. Wind on the water like moon skins.
Silence swimming towards me. I can keep this up for months.
The entire world exists in this web; there is no end to silver.
Sometimes there are voices and other dangers. From the deep green
I sense death and another existence. Sometimes I can see moon
and wonder if it has any other purpose. The grass planet clings,
millions of visions collide and re-assemble and drift aside. Is
there anything else? Once I saw a human hand ahead of me.
It was so lonely in the silver weave. It had nothing to do.
Perhaps these stones belong to it; relics, ruins, toys.
At three in the morning the sky has entered the water, grass stars
and pull of the moon as life repeats itself. My silence is elegant,
my mystery is in repeating a riddle millions of times.

THE MAN WHO THOUGHT THAT HE WAS A GARDEN

Tulip flame, poppy flush and sunlight like a skin.
Coming here to find oneself and discover between seasons
ideas of ghosts. Between the summer house in winter
and the shed's stench of apples and sacking we flow,
we revive, we settle our territory. Each year it is
exactly the same; it is totally new; storm damage
and beneath the pond's surface sinews, shades, slaughters.

At dawn each bird begins again. I am amazed by herons.
I gather ancient children into a cluster of lupins.
Beneath snow you cannot know what I am doing, can you?
Winter is a fist and I hide, clasp the ice,
concealing, the aconites hinting, whisper of snowdrops
in the hand of Spring; yielding, opening, shocking.

THE MAN WHO THOUGHT THAT HE WAS A BLUE CHAIR

Facing autumn, the window to the cliff, ocean pathway;
at this season the gold deepening and also the stubborn tourists
still trekking as if they had nowhere to return to. Now
is the time to think it over again, restore values, get it
in proportion. On Mondays I am the blue chair with a new
poem in the head. On Tuesdays I am the blue chair with
visitors to prepare for. Then I drift again; the garden is
ready to die, the words of old songs gather again.
The postman when he plods up the drive is dreaded.
I will sit it out even when he swears about the catalogues.
The kitemakers' convention was cancelled by storms.
The person you are calling knows that you are waiting.
Words begin again. They sit down to explain.

THE MAN WHO THOUGHT THAT HE
WAS A DECLARATION OF HUMAN RIGHTS

I am running down the middle of my time and you cannot,
will not, shall not stop me. I am in the middle of my
never-ever-cannot-ever-stop. I see you cannot see
me in the midst of all these headlines. You cannot catch
me in the hide and seeking storm. I cut the great beast's
head in two and sink my teeth into its looms of lust.
Oh I am running in and out of hoops of fire and dazzle.
Your hymns do not reach out to me. Your drums catch
fire in futile orchestrations. Your widows scream in fields
of ice. I run between the rat and hare and see the priests
impaled on bells. Oh I am running loud and high and seize
the night. We see the refugees dancing between the landmines,
setting the UN building on fire, building an ark of grass.

THE MAN WHO THOUGHT THAT HE WAS RAIN

Ghost-blowing across these winter fields, ruins on the run;
sometimes sudden as if eels pealed silver pores, the
light lifting, land and sky both hauled, hunted, the birds
driven to shelter and the roadways dancing, headlights cutting
through the downpour crevices, the collapse of detail, crack
of definitions. I could be lost in this. Between the stones
of ancient buildings, between the incised epitaphs, between
the refugee camps and the political conventions and the film
crew waiting for survivors; the rain that changes
everything and nothing, the secret fields and the charmed
gardens. I am the emperor of rain, the god of downpours,
the eraser of messages on slate and seaside slumbers.
I shock the stones to blossom. I season silence.

THE MAN WHO THAT THOUGHT THAT HE WAS SECRETS

Ever since the first story told to him by his mother
in that voice of wind and stars and autumn orchards, ever
since the teacher had seized language by the throat
and squeezed it past bleeding into a silent rope, ever
since the wasp sting had pained him past screams
and the image of a man skinning a rabbit had banged
on his being, ever since the nakedness of magazine girls
had drummed up his legs and whisked his testicles,
ever since the empty church had let dust fall
on the faces of saints and the lock had turned on God,
ever since the words in the letter said 'can't we
simply be friends?', he had perceived his small and quiet
position on this planet of silences, secrets, nests.

THE MAN WHO THOUGHT THAT HE WAS HIS MOTHER

Standing so silent in the room of mornings, smell of
shoes and toast, the windows wide with dawns, here in
the nest again. I slip on an early hour. I dress in a
Monday. I make a good morning and lay out all the words
before packing them. In each room there is memory and old
times and ghost jokes. Riddles and when I hoover I get
out the joke book and take care not to destroy the

catch-phrases. At mid day the house always sways.
A little bit of what you fantasy and don't let the
bugs get to you. The flowers are in the vase. The
vase is in the flowers. The television is under the flowers
and at five o'clock the world becomes news. I do
not know what I would do without you near, so near.

THE MAN WHO THOUGHT THAT HE
WAS SOMEONE ELSE'S DREAM

What to do with the tree sleeping in the spare bedroom?
I thought it was a branch of beech but now it inhabits
the entire room with birds in its hair. The stench of nests
and the creak of lice. What can it mean to be, be to mean,
the tap tap of terror when the spider hops onto your
nose in the midnight green and all I can say is winds?
The lady in the dawn garden breaks up pots
and changes the plants yet again. She had thought this was
that when all the time it was a feast for snails and the
small frogs get in her hair and with a toad up your
nose it is difficult to make any sense at all of
war and church magazines and dog fleas and why does
the dream not know who it belongs to; or is it me?

THE MAN WHO THOUGHT THAT HE WAS A SILENCE

Not to say. No voice. Letting it go. Beyond
vespers and promises in the coiling dark. Sometimes I hover
in the damp grass of the composer's head. I think it is Elgar
who really wants to be off to the races but his wife has told
him that he must complete another page before noon.
The silence says not yet. The silence says consider
the immensity of the Malvern Hills and why is it that
riding a bike reminds one of green lakes and women's
biceps? Silence of the owl eye. Silence of the torn
dream. Silence of the sunset bough and the letter
in the drawer. When I am silence I sit by
the window and look across three counties and wait
for the bells of Worcester cathedral to beat time with angels.

THE MAN WHO THOUGHT THAT HE WAS A MIGRAINE

In the head, splinter-dazzle, locked-in light, drum
dragging you down and the words have become gristle. Eyes
on fire and what is that cold caught between the idea
and the expression of the idea and the tide of nausea
that rivers in the beak? Owl, falcon, eagle;
what storms do I ride, what deserts surpass?
Flying between the split stars and ruined planets
I am also crab, spider, octopus; clenched in
a nest of stings, a vulture hour, a
forest of wounds. Words won't. Ideas hack. A
mirror would kill. In the hole I cling to
roots, scabs, scuttering scales. The kite of
childhood blazes. This roar of lost dawns.

THE MAN WHO THOUGHT THAT HE WAS A POEM

There was a moment when words made this other meaning.
It was not easy. It was a cave painting. The secret
gardens. The beast in the hungry forest. The hunters
coming out of the darkness. Bison, deer, boar; the
stockade of shadows, the voice of violence.
The figures at the doors, the alphabets of fascism,
the dance of dead dialogues. Within this another
language, another drum, a bell to tell, the poem
in its nest of metaphors, in its tree of allusions,
the enduring shock of truth, the song out of
silence, out of screams, out of sanctuary. I am
words. I am singing. I seed expectation. I am poem.
At five in the morning I begin another psalm.

THE MAN WHO THOUGHT THAT HE WAS A CHURCH BELL

To call you, to warn, to inform your sense of God
and his terrible whisper. Across these centuries, these
fields of generations, these waves of history. To call
you to these expressions of faith or frailty, these
falterings and faults and this leaping language. In
your solemn summers and slow autumns. In your
wild winters and the temptation of spring. How

I call, howl, haul you in. To time, to toll,
to speak in tokens. To summon your seasons of
love and birth, dementia and death. To cover your
dreams with diagrams of desire and destruction.
To peal you to prayer and conformity. I am
that other hymn, that other voice; listen.

THE MAN WHO THOUGHT THAT HE WAS A RED VIOLIN

There have been those moments, there have sometimes been
those moments when at the actual moment, rather than
before or after, rather than prediction or recollection, when
the silence opens its bud and there is a scattering of all
that has been before, an unfurling of the sound into
the awaiting space, the room, the house, the property,
the field, the entire world of knowledge and being and
evidence of identity and then, yes, then, at this
second I thought I was going to be a dancer,
a drum, a poem, a desert dawn, a daffodil
on fire, a ferret dream, a tablespoon, an
entrance sign, a seashell sigh; whereas
all the time I knew, I knew I was a red violin.

THE MAN WHO THOUGHT THAT HE WAS A SHOE

This way and that and sometimes straight ahead. Best foot
forward and all that sort of thing and sometimes the slim
fit of an almost naked lady who is dying to be daring.
Sometimes in dreams of reality I tap dance to doubt,
and the marching of children makes me miss a step. Dazzling
silver or dotty blue, spitting slick or laces broken I'm
this way and that and sometimes under the bed and sometimes on the
run, the track, the slippery path to goody you know
who. Silent as white. Still as satin. Soft as polish.
Stanley Kubrick should have made something of me.
Spats are back and sin is in and it's a long time since I
popped out of the box. Sometimes too quiet. Left off.
The spare pair. The garden pair. Cracked up. Unfit.

THE MAN WHO THOUGHT THAT HE WAS A GRAND PIANO

After the disintegration of language, the days of rain and flames,
the faces imploding, the gesticulating mirrors,
the windows looking in, the voices of toys speaking out,
this solution, this grand enterprise, to entertain the hurling
angels, to strike dumb the men in white, the women in white,
the dreams in white, the children in white, the white questions.
Eyes of the clock. Secret of the sheets. Meanings of the necklace.
Paper bag faces splitting open or sucked by the machine.
Silent as snow. I think I know a tune or two.
Or is it a cough? A percussion of whispers. A psalm
too soon. A triumphant concerto. The black notes telling
us. The shock of a single note and then this silence.
This is the way I like it. Polished. Perfection. Lid down.

UNCOLLECTED POEMS

The Closing of Days

1 DAYS

He assumed that the days would continue.
He could do nothing with them.
Suicide was pointless. How could he throw it
all away, abandon his reality, question existence?
So days flew past and over like improbable birds with
deep orange beaks and startling squawks and other voices.
There was nothing about such birds in the books he read.
There was no communion with these things. There was a
vast and continuing simplicity of knowing that he was alive.
The food to be consumed. The wine to be carefully selected.
The valley to be admired. The visit to the small hotel
above the lake still a bell in his memory. His
wife somewhere else with a new life, a new man,
the letters torn to shreds before they were even written.

2 THE JAGUARS INHERIT THE CAFÉS

He was sure that this was wrong. The
stupid man must have written it down incorrectly.
The word should have been 'inhabit'. To 'inherit'
would call for legal necessities, documents, lawyers
who would surely have wished to dispute or at least
hold up the procedures whilst every hour dripped money.
No, it was wrong. The writer was too hurried. Whereas
the scene of jaguars roaming between the tables, the
diners, the flower arrangements, the wine coolers, the
gold-painted chairs, the music of conversation, was
most pleasing. Where was it? At what time did these
cafés open and what prices did they charge? Could
he perhaps meet a friend there? A lover?

3 AH YES, THE SILENCES BEGIN TO DANCE

He began to consider his mother, her
last days, the way in which her words peeled from her mouth
in short movements, creating a rhythm, a momentum
beyond the meaning (she had lost logic years before).

Now he remembered how this momentum gathered into a rhythm
of such proportions that his mother began to sing, to
clap her frail and lovely hands, to raise her voice
higher and higher within the spiral of the song. And
then she stopped, closed it, finished it, and as if
determined to receive some echo or answer back she
closed her eyes. Ah yes; the silences begin to dance.

4   MOURNING BECOMES ELECTRIC

And you should know, my friend, my beloved
that the wind betweeen the trees reminds us always
of autumn and her cool declarations not to be poetic
for the boats in the harbour are full of tragedy
and the priest in his room worships his teddy bear
and what was written in your ear was love, true love.
The bells wait for summer dawns, for deaths and
weddings. Once in Spain an entire funeral procession
was held up by the San Miguel beer truck. The
driver was so drunk he drove over a cat. The owner
attacked the driver. The driver ran into the church.
Women wearing huge hats laughed so much they
dropped their handbags. The men all felt thirsty.

5   THE COUNTLESS SMILES

As dawn returns to the harbour all night walkers
who have wandered the cliff tops descend to small cafés,
to look into the eyes of a new day, another bag of reality,
the sea's odour in their eyes and hair and on their skin.
And the slim waiters serve them coffee and fresh orange juice
and breakfasts smelling of respect and order and normalcy.
They all long for a revolution, a tramp to emerge
from the waves, a drunk sea captain, an escaped
prisoner from the moors, a madman from his tree.
Instead the radio begins to play its banal tricks,
the sun rises on small cottages and tiny lives,
and in the cemetery the stones stick up like
fabled fish.

6 WHOEVER COMES GOES

It is a fact, my friend, these
lives add up to very little. A tragedy here, a
revenge there, a remarkable failure in the morning
and a successful roar in the early evening.
We observed this, we ignored that. We said
love was on our side and waited too long.
All the sad emperors of history wade out
at the small harbour wondering if their palaces
are safe, their rules respected, and why they
still envy their simple gardeners.

7 RAIN DANCE BEGINNING

Not a narrative. No longer the pre-Columbian dream
gone dead in the head, ghost dances inside their hogans,
the small town gathering its disorderly compassion to celebrate
what music and dance and the camera can catch. The broken hope
of its history. The crazy poetry of rain dance beginning
between truckers and beer sellers and lonely history hunters.
And the desert on all sides, saying keep out, forget me,
stay in your own air-conditioned century, don't take to the beginnings
of tracks. This Sunday heat beginning its own dance.
The faces of the dancers hardly exposed, giving away nothing,
as if their minds had entirely flown.

8 WITH WHAT WORDS OF KNOWLEDGE

Without inspiration the poet sad within his afternoon,
the river where it always has been and the books unread
on the shelf and the travel plans not yet ready for discussion.
A new year and the countryside freezing green in its stone.
He was still unsure what to do; phone, write, stroll, sleep.
To spend an entire day pressed into dreams. But the phone
calls him, the dog takes him out, he is forced to salute
the bright new. It is only in his diary that he gets it
said, with what words of knowledge, of self, of being,
of leaping between planets, of scowling at silences,
of wishing to get it said inside the knowledge.
Too much light. The Christmas decorations lying in

the boxes now, curled up, fizzled tricks and the long
month with brilliant early afternoons. A gold too bright
for autumn and yet not spring. The first snowdrops
forcing up their huge frailties.

9   AFTER THE LEG SHAVER'S CONVENTION

To assume that this is all. To believe
in the silences between trumpet solos.
To wait for the doors of the universe to
close, slowly, each one in turn. All your
life the houses of the famous dead falling
apart and the hermit finding his hymn
in the tallest winds. After the leg
shaver's convention we sent off postcards
to friends, took in a show, and finally
purchased early editions to see ourselves
on show. So calm. So cool. Our
wisdoms astounding the real world.

10   SHE ONLY WANTED TO SAY

He was there to be memorable.
To be within it. To be essential. And she,
clearing her throat, positioning her body, making
ready to face the faces, dedicating herself to the
declaration, now began to cough badly, so badly,
so awkwardly and loudly and constantly that the sweat
on her face made her look like a cheap glistening doll.
How could there be magic in this?
How could this be memorable, how could he be within it,
how could this be essential? So he got onto the small
yellow bike inside his head and rode off across fields
of deep and meaningful green never thinking of his
actual life (the gift, the calling, the responsibility)
for a moment.

11 FOR YOU AND I HAVE

For you and I have been there. Believing
what others have forgotten we must dream for them.
The clatter of rumours and the origination of poems
Each day trying to attempt, longing to encounter, the
embrace of abstraction, the hurling of values. If
the very old repeat only what is respectable, if the
young are trained to be logical, how will it begin?
The dancers hide beneath cedars with their music.
The musicians play cards spreading lies about
the composer, the conductor, the empty concert hall.
The critic holds his wine glass up to the light
hoping that somebody will notice him and speedily
arrive with a magnificent vintage. Meanwhile,
meanwhile.

12 THE HOSPITAL GARDENS

He closed the curtains slowly. Slowly he took
the curtains in his hands to close them, to lose the view,
to hide himself within the room of quiet.

No words were needed. He held each curtain and slowly
as a tired man shuts out a noisy day he drew
the material across the view of the gardens.

His hands were gentle, deliberate, careful as they held
the quiet material although his mind was noise, a
noise of splitting tin, of ancient sea chains.

He saw the view of the garden disappearing. He was
in control. It was his act. It was his decision.
The quiet of the room spread across his shoulders.

He closed the curtains slowly. Slowly he took
the silence in his mind, the closed day, the
finished view, the material like moth wings.

He closed down the day. He veiled it out.
he felt the huge space of the room, the
silence of a planet behind him.

He dared not turn round. He dared
not turn.

Lightning Elegies for Don Quixote

I think poetry
I think it must
Stay open all night
In beautiful cellars
Thomas Merton, *Cables to the Ace*

1

Declarations, cold thoughts, comforts; the wounds
of issue getting through steel days and
hopeless nights;
dancing the unknown counterpoints, sustaining the bent
images:
   truth fugue in the mornings
   and drummed ritual at night:
absurdity of the worldly
exposed
in the highlife of
the Mexican flea.

2

Let them all come out in the mornings
to proclaim
the freedoms they have won:
the monk singing silence,
the poor sucking the juice from autumn,
gods searching for answers
in the meanings of prayers.

3

As Prologue
we should take our man riding through fields of mental snow:
fat sun in fat sky with big mountains:
and don't miss a mosaic of dice
rattling in his eyes:
he sold a private river to the group of old women.
He sold a tall green tree to a boy with broken flowers.
He sold a picture of sunrise to a blind man.
He sold a solid gold gong to a deaf woman whose hair
was white with waiting.
All this was transacted on setting out,
sworn on a moon stone
and exchanged for a page of eternal memory.
What a man needs is a good Prologue.

4

Without the slightest fear of damage
he raids the unspeakable season
of famous love,
pinning hope to the smallest ray of sun
which has somehow got hitched between two
mountains
that he can never reach this night.

5

My prayer tonight is a slow dance, a mental shuffle:
no event is ever wasted, nothing can be totally lost:
waiting for the white rain or the bald angel
who bites his nails because he is too terrified to
dream again.

6

When he was old he wanted to be.
Often the days passed him by and
nothing was something. The tables
gathered dust. The chairs grew in
the earth. Stones came up in the

rain. Voices were slow insects that
bit you and took your blood. Even
literature was hollow and those
steel spun soliloquies grew in
the head until one could hardly
think. Some days it was best to
merely sit there and when the
fat tourists came by with their
gestures it was easy to gape
like a tired soldier who
had lived through worse than
hell. Time became a turd and
the bald angel lost his
singing voice. He wasn't even
good for a lie.

7

But NOW;
        speak of the celebrated idea,
speak to it,
        VERY loud: let everyone hear you;
let there be no confusion:

insist

on a season   of
fury.

8

Remembering the mad;
they lost what they never found:
considering old gods;
they were given what they never gave:

the memory
of women
who came to the river
every day

searching for water
before
it was
born

9

After a night sleeping out
beneath
        old ideas
he gets up and goes
               like a slick wind
that knocks the breath out
leaving the skin
hot and cold at the same
time:

our hero with the same sun returning
and the world like a warm loaf
to be bitten
when he finds his dentures.

10

In the city
standing in the rain
of faces
climb into the air
with your voice
insist on your season
of fury
before they break your
legs and drag you back:
               as
you fall

(feel the kicks, pain, breaking zeal)
you will be aware
of old grass

slowly clawing
at the
legs

of public buildings.

The Memory of Rooms

1
They are rooms:
people are   floors   doors   spaces   intervals   the inside situation
keeping inside the outside situation that they know about but do not
think about and do not see:

they do not sit inside thinking about the outside
directly; it is
only
if voices get here   come   entering without emotions   without
their owners:

they get here without form yet formal,
coming in front of their masters like disobedient dogs:

within the room we are   doors   spaces   intervals   the interior values
keeping our eyes on the mouths and the other eyes and the mouths and the
walls enclosing all these ideas:

each brain might be called a little bottle:
fragile   certain colours   certain odours   the sort of thing
yellow faced detectives like and want to drain:

between the words   doors   spaces   intervals
messages that just survive   getting through   allowed:
reason like a rodent operator   tall conversations   snapped-off ideas
dream mirror
fossel rock

smart death
balloon idea
red angels
          fly away again:

at night   very late   it is really day:
the noise is over   marriage and festival
gather round the green balloon:

stripped air   mirrors   divide.

2

Every time the same inquisition
within the rooms he was
standing within the idea
every time the same:

he could never get here
without the grey voice

even the ceiling
was a vision
of intention
stained
veined
gone wrong
off form.

3

Two hundred years later the same room with
everything changed for the new
ideas have to be expressed in the size
only removing a few of the older characteristics
we would not have to stay there for ever
ideally the children's room would be on the other side
houses like this in picture books
we have decided it reminds us too much of our fathers
house was plundered beneath sea and winds

the deeds were made out to be old
as she came out we saw on her face
the corner hid her for a moment
room without a thought
room without a red angel
room without a smart death
room without an agony
room without a bride
room without a balloon
room without a festival
there is no there is no
there is no there is no
room to breathe in here.

4

For once it might be different
talking
saying
expressing:

her body   mirror   white
if he and her in the room
her body
could get up stairs and
just ask her and
see   her body   must be
a bed with her body   his dream
without the others
downstairs their voices
wounding air
the bed   mirror   white
and after
returning to the words
for once it might
come   off   it   might
talking
saying
fossil rock

come over and
on the bed
come over and
on the floor
come over and
the mirror falls away the dress falls away the voices fall away the skin
come over and
DOOR OPENS LIGHT COMES IN VOICES COME IN THEY ALL
 COME IN AND CATCH THEM
UP TO THEIR NECKS IN WORDS
      SOCKETS
      SMART DEATHS
come over here and get a look at:

she was beautiful
thirty years ago –
    he said.

5

Bury
the room
in your fat
black year book
in your moon cupboard
in your voice bag
in your crooked jar of sleep:

it will not love you
it will not ask you questions
it will not remember you
it will not dream you:

the room is river now or stone or stone:

bury the room.

Silence
In Memory W.H. Auden

1

Land sinking in its own time: the complete
history and meaning. Sea yelp between the old
blue thunder and smallest creatures. Existing
beneath the rip of birds; their skid-scream. And
the perpetual returning of fears. Winters hurling
the notion of precisions; the slow screams of decay.
Wide days with skilled doubts and the beach swallowed
by the wind. Walking here with your future and your
childhood locked into some secret hymn. Aware of the
creatures, the intervals, the tall days of conversation
following remembered ghosts. Everything changes within
the circle and the circle that you recognise does not
change at all. Time-spinning mercy cradles what never came
and the songs hide in the old wound of rocks like broken
angels. It is not possible to forget any of this. Tokens
are taken and returned in the rhythm of these tides.

2

Buildings: keeping their own time whether you leave
them or they leave you. The construction of lives and
white silences. That slow procession you inherit and
inhabit. If you escape the laughter the garden will
wait to present its slow murders. Nobody expects you
to die like this. Friends are the enterings, the lawns,
the drive; each day parades its small festivals and
search for events. Each night cat crawls round you
and sleep is a rush of stolen time. The birth bed
and sick bed and love bed and death bed. These stairs
like swollen clocks that your days rewind. And
children; more than anything else; measuring the past
in their present. Long after you have left the same
walls of disorder and chance; the same talk of revision;
the same intervals collected: slim intervals: new suns.

3

Land came back to us. We did not go mad and nobody danced.
It was like laws seen through old river ice. The low moan of
constant recognition. A seed held in the winter land that we
sensed must be waiting. A psychic walk through the disturbed
ruins. What we take from this music must be a signal of the future
more than hereditary, cradled in the family pain with words
like sealed tokens and those spoken wounds. The delight if it
can be expressed is new grass over the old stones, the agile
pebble roar in the sucked tide, small vow pressed into the
palm of identity. Land gives us this and takes back new form.
We begin in it, a folded territory and strange rivers we had
not seen before. The map does not say this. The guide was never
here. The release of the things experienced defeats manner and
moral and bondage. A song of kite flying in the mind.

4

It cannot be said anymore in the memory. Old frog dies
in the blue grass. Old horse runs in the yellow fields.
Moon jarred, the old rose folds its broken music. And it
is not words. The glass sentences will never do it. Pages
fall across the mind like childhood thunder; the trees
have disappeared. Famous alterations to one's life catch
us on a mission to eternity and the moth will show us how to
die again. We gave our friends those gifts. We were so sure:
those hidden bells. It was another day. We were not lost.
We hid them slowly in those ruined years. Forgive the book.
Sell the dream. Fat ladies dance so certainly and the smallest
creatures die in their dreams.

How the Silence Stacks at Ellis Island

I

What is white bread? What is banana?
'H' is for heart problem, 'L' is for lameness.
You cannot hide the heart problem, it never goes.
Sometimes you can hide the lameness by keeping
within the crowd, clinging to the queue, using
your baggage to bow you down.

Five hours of questioning and then set free
to the coal, the cattle, the railroad
or detained until the eyes lose
that redness.

In freezing dreams the EYE MAN spies.

II

Twelve million landings here
and each arrival more like a farewell.

With what language do we now describe
the silences?

A wooden hat box filled with fears,
a field in Ireland for ever
fixed in the grip of this glove.

A pathway or a small room
or the eyes of those left behind
to sit between the hours of questions,
the assembling of a new identity.

In freezing dreams the EYE MAN spies.

III

Entire days spent on deck
between blankets and rags, wind
and shit and the mouths that could
no longer tell the stories.

Later a game of graffiti
to keep one whole, to name
the blame, to say that you
were here

about to disappear.

What is white bread?
Is 'future' food?

In freezing dreams the EYE MAN dies
and we see Annie Moore from Ireland
telling her story.

Thunder Elegies
3 memorials for Thomas Merton

1

Who would in dense and ragged night
get up to write these wounded fictions
upon mind's ice,
giving these stars, these ceremonies; a room
caught in skins of the moon;
the mercy with folded wings,
the wind with busted teeth.
the page as prophet.

2

Appalled by truth's etiquette
the old gods forge their dances
and the snowman becomes king for five days:
poetry plans its beautiful elegies
in sequenced ruins:
the conversations of ancient eyes
turn in on the territory
of the known mad.

3

In Dharmsala, with the Dalai Lama, in a moment
of sun, you both looked like prizewinners; the light
across your faces a private light; robes as ritual:
do you dream in mosaics now,
or
has the thunder just begun?

After Reading Yoshioka Minoru

The Four Monks

After six days of snow
four monks wait in a field.
The white sun sees the old woman
and her skinny boy as she stops
to listen to them.
The five trees observe as the local poet
spends half an hour in their company.
The river, nearly hidden, senses their conversation
when three school girls fold their arms and try not
to giggle.
All day the four monks explain the snow, the sun, the
five trees and the half hidden river.
This is what monks are for; they know not only
the questions but the answers also.

And again that night, wrapped in their own tight winds,
they find it very hard to sleep. The question tormets them.
Who will explain their deaths?
Who will open the earth for them?

Details from A Pictorial History of Medicine

1

Did you ever see such ugly heroes?
Einstein with Charles Steinmetz,
vaudeville hams,

              mystic hucksters:
god they look bad!

                Albert with a big
black hat, coat like a tar barrel, a
human oil slock:
and Charles, lop-sided, hunched, blunt
crew cut,

              body of a broken memory:
and the door or whatever it is
behind them
leading to or from the unforgettable
problem:

              a sort of silence bleeds around them
and one understands why Oppenheimer
looked so out of it
standing in
the desert.

2

A montage of two superimposed photographs projects four specific
areas of great medical progress in the twentieth century: surgery,
biochemistry, atomic medicine, space medicine. Shown are
radioactive tracer apparatus used to locate brain tumours, patient
wearing a numbered, circled cap to locate brain areas, a
distillation column attached to other laboratory glassware.

3

Have a heart.
Fibreglass is
good for you.

4

Electronic switch on a single beam
shows
Freud's consulting room: 19 Berggasse, Vienna:
The Persistence of memory
in a laboratory
dog.

5

Finally it is good to know
that in 1809
Dr. McDowell successfully removed an
ovarian tumour
from a Mrs. Crawford who sang hymns during surgery.

6

From the bucket
in a corner
a
slackening

        cry.

NEW POEMS

Selling Father

Last words do not last and anyway
I was not there and in reality neither was he.
Now other sounds rearrange our idea of him;
his desk chair, the summer house door, the folding over
of a Sunday newspaper, match striking, lawnmower.
This is not about him but our going without him
as if somehow he had left us these ways. It does not
work as we might imagine. His desk chair swirls just
as the robin spears a worm. The summer house door
conceals the sleeping tramp. This is not about him
but us. The Sunday newspaper catches fire and
as I stash the Christmas tree base an odour
of summer lawn emits a little gasp. Dead flies.
This is about how we keep the dead things alive
and entertain ghosts in the smallest acts. Suddenly
it is about our own last words that we wish to
confide, our own prayers and stumbling silences.

Easter in Cornwall

In Cornwall the light collapses and begins again.
We hang all the words up at night and nest in dreams.
Sitting in the trees each morning the new day's breath.
What it is to know where endings begin?
Sometimes the bell from Zennor catches fire.
Herded in orthodoxy, let loose in fears.
What becomes of the green man in winter?
He is always there.
Again Sunday, again prayers.
Where we began is a small story. What
ever are we doing with these words?
The birds of Cornwall flying out of Easter.
Enter the boy Christ running across
his father's fields of roaring gorse.

Enter the whispers of fishermen and their great
swearing. Enter the drowned man's riddles.
Look out across this bay of wings.
In Cornwall the light collapses and begins again.
Did you see the man's hands?

It is the Rector

It is the Rector standing at the gate
searching for a beginning. 'In the beginning', he says;
He always says that and then God commences.
In the beginning the waking, the glimpse of a dream, the
hot tea, ablutions, the first prayer, cold toast.

'I do not know where love begins'. At the gate
to the glebeland; fallen wall, nettles, Quantock Hills
almost jumping in the January light, shade of
foxes and shadows, sun in winter to psalm him now.
'I do not know where the words may place us.'

Rector talking to himself again, his conversation
with angels. the low sky and clouds like fish.
Then work. Letters. Texts. Accounting these days.
Then visits. Prayers. This little life.
'Where have we come to now?'

It is the Rector standing at the gate
with a dead child to robe in words, a
slow dying for Mabel Trewin and Oliver,
a field to bless next week, another sermon
coming on. Day's end. Meat. Sky like bread.

Place of Learning

I am not a ghost. Mr. Gaster is looking out
towards St. James' steeple with his back to the class.
I sneak into a desk next to the clever boy.
Mr. Gaster plays this trick to demonstrate his ability
to exert discipline and we wait until the magic breaks.
It is all magic you see, the numbers and the way history
repeats itself and the natural world where small things
fall out of big things and everything must have a complex
name. What we wish to know is not in Mr. Gaster's books,
however. How to make a better catapult. How to create
the world's greastest stink bomb. The history of Dick Barton.
What rats really think. The problem of the bosom.
As the silence climbs behind Mr. gaster the clever boy
has written another blinking sonnet and I wait for the moment
that must always come when the question flies towards me
decorated with density and obliqueness and what always seems
to be derision. What is it all about? What is it
related to? Why does Mr. Gaster always start with me
when the clever boy is there large as life and waving
his arms about as it he had perched on a knitting needle?
Mr. Gaster waits. The entire class waits. The steeple
of St. James' church also waits. The angel bearing
the word of God waits. It is time I disappeared.

The Six Conditions

I.   That you do not kill your father
     with words
     or prayers.

II. That you leave for your children
     a memory of meanings
     rather than the actual.

III. That Cornwall
     remains
     a ship.

IV. That you do not dig up
    your father with words
    or prayers.

V. That the old remain
    as future memories.

VI. That her voice
    is morning.

How to Make an Evil Concupiscence

They dropped their voices at this point, so that we
might not hear about 'adult things', although
Latin grammar was meant to be essential to civilised life
in that without it how would we know the meaning of things?

They also dropped their voices when talking about Jews
and divorce and something that was done to the boy next door
only he woke up in the middle of the operation and his
mother ran out of hymns to sing.

Dropping the voice was also done in church a lot and
in the doctor's waiting room but that was because
we were all trying to make out what he was saying
about Richard Stone and his glass eye.

A lot of other things were 'dropped' as well;
bombs, people to be interviewed, Stalin and boys' balls
before they could become men and have women friends
and learn how to make evil concupiscence,

between getting up at the crack of dawn and working
all hours and not ever letting up and hardly ever
finding time to be alone with a woman or a girlie
magazine or bloody one-night stands.

They dropped their voices so that we might not know
and we never told them what we already sensed, dreaded, realised;
opaque distances of wet dream dawns and lies for
friends, vocabularies that buggered, truths that simply weren't.

Windows of Lonely Farms
North Devon

What we seek between broken days
and no words entering and the distance ruin.

Last time the vicar came here to call
his horse couldn't get through the snow.

He yelled out seasonal greetings and left
us in these chimes of wind.

What we saw all winter was dead
and the ice sky birdless.

When I looked out at the orchard's devastation
I saw the fox between lichen and hollows.

The fox stared back and saw nothing
and saw not even where I would have been.

From here you can see where the byre burnt
and the hump of a stone where they killed the pigs.

When the fox looked up I could see his yellow
mind but he could not scent my hurt at all.

In summer the rose still climbs as if there
could be a wedding. The distance is ruin.

October is lonely. We enter dead nests.

Good Friday

The Christmas wreath becomes a crown of thorns
hung above a stack of logs
that won't be used this winter.

A waiting sky as between showers
those who will walk in witness
wait for the man and his cross.

How many years shall we do this
and with what changing words
turning over this story?

The silver birch begins to pour its
glory above dead daffodils
as we enter small gardens

removing weeds
and
stones.

This

This is not writing on the water
but deep reeds revealed between tides.

This is not belief
but hymns hewn out of faith.

This is not a miracle
but our interpretation of humility.

This is not the word of God
but our idea of God's idea.

Between this and that, monsters,
silences, the poets.

The Easter Snowman

The Easter snowman wears a crown of thorns.
The adults are amazed: 'what have we taught our children?'

His button eyes, his fir cone nose,
the Christmas wreath rammed onto his skull.

What have we taught our children between gales and bells,
and a language beyond belief
and messiahs stretched out to die?

Listening to Lazarus

What's he got to say now?
Dreaming of the next death when
there will be no words to rescue him
and earth bulges from his gob. Sometimes
he bashes on about angels and lights
but I think it's all in his head
and the heat of silence burns in him.
Nobody listens much now. He's
said all he's got to and we wait
to shut him up again because
it's driving us mad. Jesus Christ;

I wish it had never taken place!
It makes you wonder if it was all
it was made up to be. Now we
keep hearing of all the other
miracles, the risings up and healings;
the certainty of things lies in
shreds. What next? Lazarus;
he keeps in a corner now, head down
and says we'll have to accept his word.
The dogs won't go near him and when
it's summer now that he's given up eating again
you can see right through him.

After Closing

After closing she dances with one of the chefs.
They both remain in their work clothes; she in her
perfect black and white, he in his chef's hat and gown.
At the piano the other chef turns out a tune or two
at the upright. It is as if this were the only way to slow
down, to recover identity, to forget the bloody food
and the dutiful dialogue and the wine snobs. Now,
after closing, the lateness of night trails, the God
is thinking of inventing another dawn, trees breathe
in bird dreams, this little tune to do what love cannot.

The Dead

The dead keep company with us in dreams.
At this time of year they appear with their drums
and diaries and old clothes and want us to listen.
They wish to let us know that they too knew summer
and talks in the late garden, they too heard the owl
and knew how suddenly late August had become harvest time.

They are in our dreams because we too are content with this,
it is what we do each November, it is the season
for accepting the condition of things, the far reaching
even in frivolous things, the repetition of small
wonders. Each morning we wake from these dreams and get up
to enter the ordinary and they do a bit of this too.

Not the Words

When sometimes it was not the words
in the classroom or in silences or going home
and especially in the church it was not the words
although people were mostly kind and the stories
were usually heading for some kind of resolution
and even truth, but when it was not the words
tears and tones and voices raised or the questions
that made the smallness hurt, when it was not
the words and even if you could get to talk
to God there were things you were meant to do
and belief was not the words and singing in the
same way and walking slowly and whispering jokes,
and sometimes it was not the words or letters or
diaries or famous passages or riddles or whatever
the Book of the Dead meant and ghosts were
rather the same as angels, when it was not the
words because machines could make the rich
go round but silence was golden and when the
old began to cry it never was the words
but the being without the words that
said so much and hurt so loud. Amen.

Haunted

I have just come in from the day. There is
nothing in it for me. There is no pity out there
and the words simply stay at their stations.

Once there was a reason for sun and legs and
fields with bells. Now I am in a corner
of a silence in a closed.

There used to be names and anecdotes
and even letters. Once a telephone.
The garden took itself away and stones.

At the top of the hill there are dead
birds and the smell of pencils. The milkman
has a whistle in his head.

The radio tells me about other people.
I gave up the newspaper so that I could
die. It is a long time since I did that.

An End to Angels

The angels have gone away and now inhabit
the places where our dreams cannot reach
and our vocabularies will not be.

We do not have the songs for them
neither do we have enough flowers and promises
to get them to return.

We tell the priests to stop their ancient
performances and that bells won't work this time
and to hell with dancing.

All we can do is wait
as the children continue to play
and the animals in the zoo
go about their
surviving.

A Hymn Might Have Done

He had a way of saying it, of doing it in words,
of taking you within the wisdom of the thing that
went beyond the words as measures of meanings.
Then there were those silences; shawls, pardons,
haltings as if we all needed to catch our
identity and get up to the moment as the words
had gone ahead, thrown down a glory or a threat.
A hymn might have done or another prayer or
somebody breaking into a laugh or a dance. Then
he was off again and we were off the hook and
roaring towards another light, another leap between
the comforting and the outrageous and the ruined.
It was like juggling candles and catching riddles
and recognising that the present is always distant.

Chasing the Last Days

Chasing the last days
can you ever find the words
hidden under a hill?

The vicar almost sets
himself aflame in a
mosaic of miracles.

The storyteller seeks a
charmed ending even
before he speaks.

Daffodils gather together
like shy girls
before a dance.

Saying goodbye can
sometimes become
almost hello.

We are Not Here

We are not here. We are in nowhere.
We are lying in the sheds of our beds
between paper days and our father's voices.
We are sitting in the wind with our toys
and the skipping songs and the naughty words.
We rubbed out the teacher years ago but
his voice keeps coming back and there is a
place where his hand keeps climbing up.
There is also a puffin and a seagull and
a pig called Susie. We are not here
and in the trees and in the playground and
in the silence when the adults put out
the lights and say longing things. We
are in nowehere and always there and
tucked between births and deaths
to make a meaning of our names.

This is the Duke on Monday Mornings

He does not like this. He does not know where to put Mondays.
There are no visitors to the garden. There is no-one to pee on.
The Duchess sleeps it off, keeps herself busy with dreams.
The Duke sniffs dankness. On Mondays he wears a green
tie and a green jacket. The boiled egg bleeds over him.
Stained purple he remembers the piano and chops up a chord
or two before the tears arrive and the stench of nanny.
Where did nanny go? She left him a bar of soap
and boiled sweets and a kite. The view from his bathroom
(not hers) is cloudy with ghosts. He can see nanny
and the huge pram and the dog that was later crushed
by the Daimler. He can see his parents
parading with two bishops from Africa. The bishops'
cloaks blaze against the deep green of England
as if they walked within a fire, flames of faith.
He can see a manservant swiftly approaching his father
to deliver a message from the battle field. Nothing can
now ever be the same again. They will now pray.
This is the Duke on Monday mornings; fingering
his green tie with its purple stains, whispering at the
window pane, remembering the smell of a brother.

Three Birds Off
For M. Church

It seemed a good idea at the time,
Washington in Holy Week, before
the flight home, the grass dancing and
then the gift of this clock.

'Each time the set test button is pressed,
this resets the bird melodies to the next hour's bird'.
The Birds of America Clock, birds to tell the time by;
at twelve the House Finch, at one the American
Monster Robin, at two the Northern Mockingbird;
Blue Jay, House Wren, Tufted Titmouse. Most
strange of all the Black-capped Chickadee
and the Northern Cardinal.

'To set the time turn the hand set knob in
rear of battery compartment clockwise. Insert 3
batteries. Make sure that the polarity is
as indicated!'

In England deciding upon the best place to display
this gift with its dark green frame. The Northern Oriole
about to leap, the Morning Dove placid on a plank,
the White-throated Sparrow strongly stern, the White-breasted
Nuthatch guarding at eleven o'clock.

'If pressed, you must follow the instructions above to reset
or you will not hear the correct melody
with the correct bird.'

And so it has been; three birds off and now seven.
It's twelve o'clock and the Morning Dove lets loose;
at nine the House Wren bends our ears when
the Cardinal should call. At seven the Robin
invades and we reach for our guns.

We do not hear the correct melody in our house.
We are constantly out of tune yet in time.
The polarity thing is shot through and each time
the set test button is pressed the disorder sprawls.

It seemed a good idea at the time. Now we think
of Famous First Lines Clocks, Last Words Clocks, the
Twelve Disciples Clock, Last Stand and Into Battle Clocks,
Shakespearean Soliloquies Clocks, to tell, to time us all,
to gather in our hours, to tick our tocks and proclaim
our days.

In the land of sounding clocks the battery is God.

Every Field Rolling Green
Poem beginning with a line from David Hart

Every field rolling green has its beautiful crashed aeroplane
and somewhere between ideas the children discover an angel.

When Mr. Porter died in church just before communion
somebody had noticed a robin in his words.

When father blessed the field Nurse Nunny
couldn't stop because she had to collect a sheep's head

for her dog and when her sister came from Dublin
the fields she said at night were too quiet for her to sleep.

Early or late, the fields wait for thunder again
and the cows think the sky will break.

'Fish for Fridays' says Cook, her apron
staining as she decapitates mackerel.

'Find a top C for God' says the choirmaster
his breath heavy with cider.

Every field rolling green has its beautiful crashed aeroplane
as we scatter Mr. Porter across the Quantock Hills.

All that Went Before

The view has come inside. This means
that the argument has hit the lawn
and all that was before is thunder.

Your platform shoes invent the 70s;
indulgent, flared, funky before we
knew it. Glass walls still glowing.

Step inside my dream machine baby
and I'll introduce you to Kojak
and other myths. Hats off to tennis shoes

and the silences of Gertrude Stein. She
invented us and she invents herself and
the repetitions ripple like foxglove days.

How high is a kite meant to go? Your
bedroom is a mobile and in between life
and lies the dreams highjack the stars.

When you threw me at the T.V. screen
they were singing the Alleluia Chorus in
Zulu. I simply joined in.

The Owls Inhabit the Cathedrals

The owls inhabit the cathedrals.
There may be some honesty here, wisdoms of
whispers and saints' brains hard as diamonds.
Angels in stone and wood and glass, sun and moon
passing right through them and the moods of seasons.
There may be some conclusion here, logic locked
in the holy hair of Jesus, his wing-like hands,
the consolation of candles and halos of hymns.

No trees. No rains or thunder. At night the
snowing silence, all day nests of prayers and
texts, each word flying towards a sentence
towards a meaning that changes everything.
When the people arrive they call it a miracle
or at the very best a sign. The Dean bids
them welcome and offers a place in the heavens.
You cannot get any higher than this. You can
perhaps hear the god breathing from here or
tapping his fingers to the tune of trumpets.
The owls stare down. The human look up
to them. Cherubim. Messengers. Clusters
of light in their urgent eyes.

The Animals Have Seen the Human

The animals have seen the Human
placing the dead ones
in earth;

have witnessed processions, rituals with music
and prayers, signs, stones to
keep under;

and keep their distance.

There is nothing for the animals
in this knowledge, this code, this
cradling time.

The humans do not want them here.
Finished flesh. Dead bone. Ancient
game with their idea of god.

On the hill top and in the forest
the animals know
this riddle
is ruin.

The Animals That Had Learnt

The animals that had learnt how to paint
produced blue nests in green skies. There were
no edges, no restrictions to the flying trees
the weeping humans, cultures constantly on the move.

The animals that had learnt how to write
scrawled new words on the sides of mountains;
Godgrunt. Miraclekiss. Reasonroar.
Bring back Brother Francis; we will crucify him.

The animals that had learnt how to speak
soon gave up. Their own calls and roars,
dawn songs and rattles were sufficient.
They invented their own riddles. They spoke of hidden scrolls.

The animals that had a God
observed His claws in everything. Wondered at the wounds
and the resurrection thing. Fantasised about the first egg
and the first nest.

The animals who had learnt how to form an army
sent their long distance flyers
into outer space. Angels with wings on fire.

The Darkness in the House

The darkness in the house covers
what they have said and what they have
not yet said, what is to be expressed
and what is mature in the memory, what has
been entered in sentences of composed words
and what has cut across the mind like dawn light.
The darkness in the house covers the stairs that
were essential, the chairs that made rest,
the gong in its voice, the way out towards
windows, these places where we controlled our
lives with anecdotes and lies, the eyes of
ancestors hung up to drip history.
The darkness of the house covers even
our messages, our letters, our small
scrawled vows and mothballed promises,
covers even our dreams as we walk
or dance in other rooms where there
may be sunlight and shades of the
spectacular, clockwork diamonds,
moth soft prayers and cut up psalms.

Carols

Nine women gripped in the storm lamp's lilting light
their fingers plucking the ducks, then the geese
in the igloo-glow of the outhouse.
Anne Craze with her old sock of a face
telling them of Prebble's fall from the clock tower
and then another carol 'O Holy Night'.
Liz Crew reminding them of the infant deaths
and the Punch and Judy booth catching fire at the fete
and then another carol 'O Little Town';
Miss Williams who lived with her brother talking
of the storm of '47 when they saw no-one for weeks

and the snow plough blocked the back lane until April
and then 'Away in a Manger';
the store of stories and voices and ripple of rumour
keeping them going as the feathers became a burnished pool,
the onion white of each bird's flesh and the plum stain
of the occasional wounds where the skin ripped;
'Silent Night' and memories of the October wedding
when the entire church was transformed into old rose;
Mary Wright now plucking the breast of the last goose
where flesh was almost human as she heaved
the torso onto her lap and felt the dead weight,
the wings folding back, the neck and the head laid
into deep lake of feathers, the firmness of this last bird
as the other women fell silent to observe her, sensed her
uncertainty, before Mabel Trewin commenced her solo.

Faith

Dancing without music, singing without words,
dreaming without a sleep, believing without a god;

we do this all the time, transcending the tribal
to articulate tokens and sometimes truths.

What you see is only a beginning, whispering
at eternity, recitals of light;

laughing without jokes, smiling in an empty room,
talking to the dead, trusting love;

we do this all the time;
then don't.

Eating God

And you must not eat God like that,
all at once and making noises. God is to be taken
slowly, with an elaborate spoon, each bit masticated
carefully, accompanied by a very fine wine or sometimes
bread and wine but never blue cheese, never mixed with fruit.
You must consume God slowly, preferably on a mountain top,
essentially with a vista of distant kingdoms, villages where
the sun spins gold and where there are no other voices but your own,
your precise vocabulary of doubt and need and definition and that fumbling
for a faith. Prepare a table and set a place and consume all you can,
always working away from the bones and what might have once been wings.

The Cathedral in Milan

Here are some of the thoughts on entering the cathedral in Milan
when one has driven down from Bellagio and left Lake Como and its
    tragic light
for a day, only a day; it will always be there.

The light on entering is like a bell that hangs ready to fall and sound;
the light has no sound but the shade of waiting for sound, the note that
will collapse the silence and fly out and stir the birds, the tourists with
    umbrellas,
the nuns, the cyclists, even the rich man behind the bottle of wine.

Or the light is like lace, old lace; nobody remembers who made it but
it is drenched in prayers and ancient music and attempts at mystery and
knots of revelation; lace like an old dance, an inherited deceit,
a rib of fiction, a narrative of saints, a fold of fable.

Or the light is its own voice or pause between voices or sentence,
before silences when the prayers and supplications grip in a riddle;

or the light is the whispers of saints who have never been understood;

or the light is the language of God transcending the knowledge of God,
feathers of faith,

or even God's closed eye.

This Poem Will Not Change Anything

He has cut himself. Winding a blue handkerchief
round his entire hand it is not possible to see how
bad it is. Of course, now it begins to rain. The entire
field smells of nettles. The axe blade darkens to black.
Sheltering we look out towards the other trees and imagine
they are heavy with rooks who want to fly out,
who must wait to escape and explore their power.
The blue handkerchief is wound tight and he grips
the wounded hand in his good hand. When the
rain stops he picks up the bill hook as if
nothing had happened and we feel the rain running
off the planet, see the whiteness when the axe seizes.

Voices in the Orchard

Voices still hang in the orchard although we have moved on.
Stench of nettles and old bark and light locked into a lichen grip.
Frog dark, toad low, a surface silence broken by children who
sensed legends here, stalking like warriors, hid jewels in nests of
white grass, never forgetting where the pig was slaughtered and skinned,
the dead bird collapsing in my hands, the ruins of poppies.
Five Chinese geese one year, seven pigs another and then the
years of waste, of wild, of straying. The trees now near
dead. The voices still there when we have all moved on.
Gasp of sharpening stone on the scythe, ring of wire before breaking,
sharding of pots and brittle wood, dead nests in the shed,
ladder ruins and the handles of buckets, beneath weed mats

sheets of window glass greening. Voice of mother calling in
the geese and Sam Frost swearing at the pigs and my own voice
as I reach for the topmost apples and call out before
dropping them. October mornings when the summer is sinking
in deep dews and we commence our familiar migrations.

Questions About the Madhouse

What they say in there?
Gone down words. Lost light words.
Whispers worrying, a gossip song stranded.

What they see in there?
Upside down and turned around and the flashes
of recognition so raw they rant.

What they remember in there?
Shoes in a line, desk lid with a rat
pinioned and the vicar fixing Sin.

What they do in there?
Squint. Squat. Inhabit the scream
and roll up into a ball of bile.

What they do to escape?
Hang themselves up. Hurl at visions.
Run at the wall until it becomes a door.

What they do for silence?
Flower dreams and dead as angels.
Dance with mirrors. Enter glass.

Somewhere

Somewhere they are picking over the words
of the man who has just died. The geese are
entering the shed for the night. The baby
returns to the dream room. The lovers look
across an orchard of sun. Rain is bending
the intricate web. Wine enters the words
and makes the tongue dance. The writer of riddles
discovers his name within a metaphor. Beds
begin their voyages in the terrible night
ward. The sniper sits down with his family.
The creature in the cage has another vision.
The postman posts his hundredth poem.
Mr. Wiseman digs up his spring potatoes.
Mrs. Wiseman hears of her brother's death
in the egg of her bed. Another dragonfly dies.

Sometimes the Words Came Off in our Hands

It isn't working. The Latin won't grow
and the algebra refuses to fire and the rain keeps
getting into my head or sex or sweat.
Other people's words. Knowledge from the outside
world. Nothing to make things happen or respect.
The voices of teachers like tireless dictators
because they have nothing to offer us but shells.
It was like this for years. It was like running
into the rain. It was like trying so hard
to get something said it burnt in your
throat. It was like two deaths at once.
At the old people's home they sat with their
toys and games and paper hats ready
for the next festival. We read to them
from a list of requests. Sometimes the words
came off in our hands.

Old Man Dreaming of Women

The only advantage of more time to sleep
is the women who arrive within the dreams.
They let you unwrap them slowly. They slip
off their songs and let you take your time.
They don't expect heroics and you can keep
repeating the best bits which are frankly
at the very beginning. They let you arrange
your fantasies and never hurry it along.
There is no reason to hurry. There are no
telephones or postmen with deliveries from
Readers Digest and the dogs never get
in on the act. There is this opulence
of taking all the time it takes. The
buttons pop open like petals. The
zipper is like a blade of grass between
the teeth. All the clocks have stopped.

Falling Through a Wedding

For Clare and Nick

We were all falling through a wedding
as you do because weddings are waterfalls
of words and bells and wishes and tidying up
between the lost years and what was assumed
and the coming together to gather up flowers.
Some of the guests were single but you still
saw them at it. Life never ends and the bits
you clipped out of the photograph have a will
of their own. Dancing was difficult because
the people you began with were constantly changing
and the music was a waltz, a tango, a march;
it was so sad, mad, formal, falling to bits.
When it came to the speeches there were other
problems because everything had to be included

whereas what you might have chosen to do
was admire the wine or sing a song or
mention a word or two about the missing
and the dead. So many who were not able.
When they left the petals we threw
were really words.

What We Are Talking About

Always gathering into a field of evening;
the orchard silent and the odour of old
conversations. So where do these vocabularies go?
The river that was once wide now a stream
packed with watercress, silence of silt
and the white horse no longer here.
Nettles, stones, sigh of the silver birch,
sunbeam flowers. Whatever words we use
these are the stories we are telling.

Dressing God

I am going to dress God in a winter dawn,
in a storm of trees, in a rampage of toys,
in a season of dialects, in a room of shoes.

When God enters the winter dawn He will see
how determined we are.
When God enters the storm of trees He will remember
the wisdom of birds.

When God clutches these small toys
it will remind him of the language of planets.

In a season of dialects God hears again
the scream of saints, the doubts of prophets,
the babble of bishops.

In a room of shoes
God hears men denying the existence of
Auschwitz.

Running Out

Today we are going to play a game;
you remember what a game is?
Here is a ball. You can feel it; it
won't explode. Go on. It's safe.
Now this is what we do to make a game.

Today we are going to draw a picture;
you remember drawing don't you?
Here is some paper and a crayon; you
can use them in any way you like.
Nobody will tell you off if the
colour begins to escape the lines.

Today we are going to sing a song;
you remember music don't you?
Here is a silence for you to fill;
you need to fill the silence with noise.
Nobody will mind you if at first
all you do is scream.

Today we are going to tell each other our names;
you remember your name don't you? Later
you will take us to the border, to the valley,
to the field where they buried four hundred names
and then you ran and ran and ran out of your own name.

Saxon Whispers
Waxham, Norfolk, June 1999

To enter pull the latch towards you, thrust down,
don't let a stench of nettles deter you.
To find this place at all is a small miracle,
turning off the road to a hidden beach or
beguiled by the image of the massive barn
or detouring to avoid cows
ambling back from milking.

Parva has long been under the sea;
the Lords of the Manor
do not know what has become of their land;
inscribed in a tide of their own meaning
they are green men now, past prayers
and parades and the naming of fields; entombed
within a sleep of seasons.

And the god, does the god remain here, believing
in these people, their flints of faith, their impossible
prayers and processional silences, still
restless within this ancient braid, this stone flesh,
this wooden bone, daylight leaking through a small
Saxon opening, the nights of winter
hovering, plunging?

'Here Lyeth the body of Thomas Wodehouse
who deceased this 21 daye of Januarye
Anno 1571'. Here lyeth some bird muck
and that stain of rain and high up small flags
of web. Here lyeth the remains of Waxham Magna
stubborn as winter sun. Here lyeth an idea
of God, an idea of after God.

To drive away now past a cottage crushed by roses,
past Parva's remaining acres, out there
the lost levels, out there St. Margaret's cradled in tides.
These lost levels of language to make the God
again, to reason meaning, to open a door
and let the light become, the voices just close enough
to deliver a decipherable phrase; then.

The Gardens

How carefully the gardens discover us;
a scatter of sun and we work until dusk
hovering over pots and matted places
where leaves and snail shells cling,
seeing what will be, sorting twine and old
seed packets and longing for the excuse to remain
in a reclaiming space, this territory of toil
and recognition, the pathway leading
towards an idea of spring.

The Confetti Maker's Cottage

Thank you for the postcard of dead horses
in a field in France taken at the time
of the First World War. I have now assembled
a collection of odd images and quaint distortions;
flooded fetes, castles ablaze, ruined stables,
closed roads, collapsed ha-has, derelict manors;
and then there are those signs to
Park Pretty or Merge and Weave, Servants Only,
You Will Drown Here, polite reminders
in a cruel world where tea rooms shut their doors
at half-past four and God is often locked up at six p.m.
Thank you for the image of Redditch at midnight

and Zennor in a month of rain.
The sign to the violin maker still stands
but the confetti maker's cottage never existed.

A Hint of Harvest

He gets up in the tired night
and enters the farmyard still ringing with moon.
If he could plant some serious words
in the top field and let them grow
and return to read their sense
when silence had become the easier thing.
If he could state these things as confidently
as he built a hedge and made the acres work;
but not words, too late for words.
Now the damage remains, the hunched house
whispering, white grass between the slabs
and as he returns to open the curtains
the hill no longer leaps, his image spies in
on him from the window glass. He sees his father
and even his grandfather and dead foxes and
birds burst by the gun. He sees the sadness
of his fact, his broken being, hears the wind's
derision as the gob of the letterbox
spews news of other tragedies.

If he could plant some serious words
and let them grow in the top field
and discover their blooms one summer,
or gather a friend to observe the wonder
and tell the priest on a good morning
how all this had value, was not lost,
was not mistaken. If he could plant
some words that would not roar rebuke,
would perhaps sing just once or twice,
would remind him of his mother's messages

as she came in from the milking; a little
laughter, the seed of a joke, something
to pass on, even a hint of harvest.

The Wall That Went for a Walk

This is a story. It is always a story. This is a story
not of a garden or a house or a path but of a wall,
the mind of the wall. It is always a story for us to believe
in when winter shuts the view and knowledge conceals
the visions of broken things and the children see beyond
the necessary rhymes.

The best gardens simmer. The best gardens redeem
the urgency that made them. The best paths race up
over the hill top. The best gates beckon beyond. This is
a story about a wall that had conformed for years
in the traditional spirit of walls. This is not a story of
falling down, bramble wars, but a fiction of ideas.

This is a story of a wall deciding to go beyond,
extend territory, explore fields and moors, seek the holy wells
and harbours, visit the dancing stones and the singing ruins,
descend to the ocean music and clamber to the crags; this is the story
that I have heard all of my life and will tell you now.

This is a story. It is always a story.

Do Abbots Live at the Abbattoir?

Searching new cities for old things,
tourists or just passers by, there are always
buildings that don't seem to mean, hide
what they are. Sometimes they are perched

on headlands where a huge hotel should be
sunning itself, like the old people's home stuck
out there all day hiding from the flames of July.
Or in a back street, behind immense shutters,
the animal experimental laboratory where even
the growls and meows are hollow. Abattoirs
set on the mountain road, hospitals for the
inept and insane near country villages, and
a fever hospital just across from the ladies
prison. And just back from the beach in Cornwall
a home for airmen and soldiers who had never
quite made it out of cockpits and bombers
in time. The hot rain still falling
and the screams of their comrades each night.
Years later a slow motion death, bits of
poems stuck like shrapnel in their heads. And
a god dressed in medals, a jolly Mr. Punch,
bellowing prayers and 'cheerio chaps', the chalice
and the whisky glass and a letter from home crunched
in the shoe box. And in Oxfordshire a mansion
set near a river, deserted still, where once they decoded
messages. In November the wind tap taps on
french windows. In January winter sun
scrawls on the terraces before huge snows.

Acknowledgements

Uncollected and new poems have appeared in the following magazines: *Acumen, Ambit, Brando's Hat, Braquemard, Fire, Headlock, The Journey, Keats-Shelley Review #14, Last Fly, Lateral Moves, Obsessed with Pipework, Other Poetry, Poetry & Audience, Rialto, Reater, Seam, Smiths Knoll, Spectacular Diseases, Stand, Staple, Stride, The Interpreter's House, Iota, The Red Wheelbarrow, Tears in the Fence, Island, Yellow Crane;*

and in these anthologies:
Completing the Picture (Stride, 1995), *Summoning the Sea* (University of Salzburg, 1996), *Voices for Kosovo* (Stride, 1999), *Horizontal* (Blue Nose, 2000)

•

'The Man Who Thought That He Was A Grand Piano' won the 1999 Berkshire Poetry Prize; 'The Man Who Thought That He Was' sequence was a Blue Nose Poetry Competition winner 2000; 'Three Birds Off' won second prize in the Keats-Shelley Prize 2000; and 'Old Man Dreaming of Women' won third prize in the Ripley Poetry Prize 2001.

•

Selected Poems first appeared in these previous collections:
The Green Dancers (Outposts), *The Burial Tree* (View), *And Suddenly This* (Driftwood), *From the White Room* (Rondo), *Somewhere There are Trains* (Headland), *Falconer* (Arc), *Last Days of the Eagle* (Oxus), *Mornings of Snow* (Greylag), *The Mind and Dying of Mister Punch* (Tern. Xenia), *Return to the Abode of Love* (Tern), *Replies for My Quaker Ancestors* (Lomond), *A Banquet for Rousseau* (Stride), *Romanian Round* (Tern), *The Rain Children* (Stride), *The All Night Orchestra* (Loxwood Stoneleigh), *Turtle Mythologies* (University of Salzburg), *Bosnia* (Tern), *Dancing with Bruno* (Blackwater), *An Alphabet of Light* (Oversteps), *The Man Who Thought That He Was* (Tern), *Conversations Before the End of Time* (Dionysia 2001).

SANCTUARY

In *Sanctuary* Lucian struggles as husband, clergyman and spiritual survivor. His parish struggles with unfinished business. The village historian sees history as messages. Prebble keeps the church clean and modern ideas out. Lucian's wife still watches for a missing son and from her damp mansion Mrs. Waley gently slides into dreams. She has a pagan item to release. The sheela-na-gig grins through ancient light and time, bringing chaos to a community already tense and divided. As fear and hostility turn into feud, another figure from the past asserts his spirit from the church where in 1232 he took sanctuary. The living and the dead cannot co-exist. Lucian begins his battle between past and present ignorance.

Sanctuary is David Grubb's fourth work of fiction. History and myth, the way people celebrate convictions and doubts, the importance of dreams and deities dominate once again. There is, as in much of the author's writing, a strong pagan identity struggling towards definition. The language is taut, intense, as befits the struggle between extremes of darkness and light.

'Grubb translates myth into personal symbols. His imagery can startle, too. Grubb continues to be intellectually challenging whether being mystical or down to earth.' *Iron*

'A distinctive presence, hallmarked by a thorough honesty of mind and feeling.' *Acumen*

'Amazing work...' *The Guardian*

Sanctuary is available for £7.95, post free,
from the publisher:
STRIDE PUBLICATIONS
11 SYLVAN ROAD, EXETER, DEVON EX4 6EW
(cheques payable to 'Stride' please)